The Condition of Music and Anglophone Influences in the Poetry of Shao Xunmei

Tian Jin
University of Edinburgh

Series in Literary Studies

Copyright © 2021 Vernon Press, an imprint of Vernon Art and Science Inc, on behalf of the author.

All rights reserved. No part of this publication may be reproduced, stored in a retrieval system, or transmitted in any form or by any means, electronic, mechanical, photocopying, recording, or otherwise, without the prior permission of Vernon Art and Science Inc.

www.vernonpress.com

In the Americas:
Vernon Press
1000 N West Street,
Suite 1200, Wilmington,
Delaware 19801
United States

In the rest of the world:
Vernon Press
C/Sancti Espiritu 17,
Malaga, 29006
Spain

Series in Literary Studies

Library of Congress Control Number: 2020938532

ISBN: 978-1-64889-168-7

Also available: 978-1-64889-051-2 [Hardback]; 978-1-64889-062-8 [PDF, E-Book]

Product and company names mentioned in this work are the trademarks of their respective owners. While every care has been taken in preparing this work, neither the authors nor Vernon Art and Science Inc. may be held responsible for any loss or damage caused or alleged to be caused directly or indirectly by the information contained in it.

Every effort has been made to trace all copyright holders, but if any have been inadvertently overlooked the publisher will be pleased to include any necessary credits in any subsequent reprint or edition.

Cover designed by Vernon Press. Cover image by Free-Photos from Pixabay.

Table of Contents

Declaration	v
Abstract	vii
Preface By Peter Dayan	ix
Introduction	xi
0.1 A short biography of Shao Xunmei	xi
0.2 Shao and Western poetry	xxiv
0.3 Shao and Anglophone influences	xxxiii
0.4 Shao and music	xxxvii
0.5 A feminist approach	xlvi
0.6 Translation policy	xlix
Chapter 1 **Shao, Swinburne and the idea of harmony**	**1**
1.1 The gathering of Shao, Sappho and Swinburne	1
1.1.1 Shao's encounter with Sappho	1
1.1.2 From Sappho to Swinburne	5
1.1.3 A poet in the making	8
1.2 Harmony as a condition of music in poetry	11
1.2.1 Swinburne's conception of harmony	11
1.2.2 The nightingale as a symbol of harmony	19
1.2.3 A shared practice: the merging of Sappho and the nightingale	24
Chapter 2 **Shao, Sitwell and "the sister of horticulture"**	**29**
2.1 Poetry as "the sister of horticulture"	29
2.1.1 Sitwell's conception of "the sister of horticulture"	29

	2.1.2 Texture and *jili* 肌理	32
	2.2 The horticulture of musical sisters	38
	2.2.1 The flower as musical woman	38
	2.2.2 Sexual consummation as a condition of music	49
	2.2.3 Garden, sexual ecstasy and possible biblical influence	51
	2.2.4 The instrumentalisation of woman's body	63
Chapter 3	**Shao, Moore and the idea of pure poetry**	**75**
	3.1 Shao and Moore in dialogue	75
	3.1.1 Shao's correspondence with Moore	75
	3.1.2 Moore's conception of pure poetry	84
	3.2 The dialogic of pure poetry	88
	3.2.1 Prose poetry and the use of dialogic	88
	3.2.2 Pure poetry as the unity of arts	98
Conclusion		105
Bibliography		113
Index		119

Declaration

This book is based on my PhD thesis "The Condition of Music and Anglophone Influences in the Poetry of Shao Xunmei".

Abstract

Shao Xunmei 邵洵美 (1906-1968), a Chinese poet, publisher and translator, has long been marginalized by contemporary criticism. His unique poetics, especially when it comes to the condition of music in poetry, remains largely unexamined. Shao aspires to reach the condition of music in poetry, which bears a resemblance to three Anglophone writers whom he applauds: Algernon Charles Swinburne, Edith Sitwell and George Augustus Moore. This book will examine how the three writers influenced Shao, and how the influences help shape Shao's idea of the condition of music in poetry.

Swinburne's conception of harmony denotes the union of meaning and sound, which greatly influenced Shao. Both Shao and Swinburne consider nature as the perfect paradigm for harmony, and they both see the nightingale as the ideal symbol for harmony. Both poets like to merge Sappho and the nightingale in their poetic practices, and the merging of Sappho—the incarnation of poetry—and the nightingale—the ideal symbol for harmony—represents an idea that poetry could reach the condition of harmony, to which both Shao and Swinburne aspire.

Sitwell puts forth the conception of poetry as "the sister of horticulture".[1] She also comes up with a notion of texture as a state of interweave in the union of meaning and sound. Shao takes in the two conceptions and adds a twist of human physiology to them. Both Sitwell and Shao consider the flower as an incarnation of music. But Shao's flower symbol often has features that allude to female sexual organs, which presents an idiosyncratic union of flower-woman. Sexual consummation with the flower-woman seems to him a way that leads to the reproduction of music in poetry.

Moore comes up with the notion of pure poetry, which requires the removal of the conception of the body in poetry. Shao assimilates this notion and attempts to reach pure poetry through replacing the dialectic of the body with the dialogic of voices. This replacement remedies the idiosyncrasy evident in Shao's poems influenced by Sitwell and frees the woman from being the instrumentalized other of "I". Moore's conception of pure poetry denotes an ideal, primordial unity of arts, in which music and poetry are one. However, Shao realizes this state could only be approached indefinitely and never be reached ontologically. Poetry and music, or poetry and other art forms, would always be in a dialogic process with no definite closure. The strategy that he

---

[1] Edith Sitwell, *Aspects of Modern Poetry* (London: Duckworth, 1934), 180.

comes up with is to play with the traversing between unity and diversity, that is, between pure poetry and poetry/music.

Preface
By
Peter Dayan

One of the many reasons for the persistent eurocentrism of Comparative Literature has been simply that the astonishing richness and diversity of literary modernism in China during the years before the Second World War has not been thoroughly explored. Even in China, it has not had the recognition it deserves. Obviously, this is partially due to reasons of political history. Certainly, the tale of China's great early 20th-century literary innovators cannot be told without an appreciation of how it ended; and Tian Jin offers a powerful narrative of the crushing of a poetic career. However, what we need most is an understanding of how poetry was developing in China before 1940, recovering the impulses, beliefs, ambitions, aspirations, optimisms, endless reversals, and equally endless creativity of the time. That is what Tian Jin provides, through the fascinating example of Shao Xunmei.

This is a great service to Chinese literary history. It is also a great service to Comparative Literature, which needs to know more about how East and West interacted in this crucial period. For the first time in the history of world literature, innovations in poetic form – free verse and prose poetry – were sweeping the entire world within a few decades; but it is not enough to see this in terms of influence or importation. As Tian Jin shows, it interacted with the literary and social forces already at work in China to produce something unique, uniquely Chinese, never static, and refracted through the powerful and vigorously opposed personalities of the poets who took up the new challenges. The poetry of Shao Xunmei really is extraordinary, not only in its quality but in its sheer difference – and its evolution. Another of the merits of Tian Jin's work is to bring out the profound workings of that evolution, particularly in relation to gender, to the gendering of voices and roles in poetry. He shows that the changes in Shao's poetic voices engaged his very notion of what poetry could be. This, as ever, he roots firmly in the historical time period in which they were occurring. But they are also very topical for us today. We have by no means finished grappling with the question of the gendering of poetic genius, and the apparently inherent tendency to misogyny of the great poetic tradition.

Nor have we finished grappling with the question at the heart of this study: the condition of music in poetry. What do poets mean when they talk about music? What definition of the word do they have in mind when they imply that their poetry is musical? The academic field of Word and Music Studies has, over the past thirty years, begun to take apart some of the more simplistic answers that often occur to us; and to show how, for at least two centuries, poets have been well aware of the subtleties, sleights of hand, and productive deceptions at work in the intertwining of the two arts. Tian Jin, building on this, adds another dimension. He shows us what happens when a concept of music created in Romantic Europe is brought into a dynamic relationship with the poetry of China, where that concept had not yet presided over the creation of a new musical tradition. The intricate relationship between the poetry and the music of Shao Xunmei cannot be explained simply by reference to the music he knew; Tian Jin tells us why.

But after all, if this study seems to me so important, that is mainly because Shao's poetry is so compelling, so attractive, so – if I may use an unfashionable word – beautiful. It deserves the attention it gets here, not only because of its historical importance in the development of world literature, but because that importance is in proportion to its poetic quality. Literary criticism cannot do justice to poetic quality unless the critical writing is itself poetic. This is especially true where the poet is likely to be unknown to the readers of the critical work. Shao is relatively little known in China, I am told. He is certainly very little known in the West. I suspect that many of the likely readers of the present volume will be people interested in world literature, literary modernism, and Word and Music Studies, who will not be able to read Shao's poetry in the Chinese original. A vital qualification to write such a book is, therefore, the ability to bring alive in English, and the translations of the original verse, the quality of Shao's own writing. This Tian Jin does superbly. His own voice is, to me, unmistakably that of a true poetic writer. His translations of Shao's poems have the power of poetry. Like his critical writing, they embody the in-betweenness of the best tradition of literary translation as of Comparative Literature. Tian Jin's text never gives the impression it is aiming to be a transparent window onto Shao and his time. It knows that to write about poetry must be to collaborate in the production of poetry, in our own time. The condition of music and Anglophone influences are at work in the writing of Tian Jin as they are in that of Shao Xunmei, and that makes this book worth reading.

Peter Dayan
Professor of Word and Music Studies
University of Edinburgh

Introduction

0.1 A short biography of Shao Xunmei

In 1906, Shao Xunmei was born Shao Yunlong 邵云龙 to a declining family of government officials in Shanghai. His grandfather Shao Youlian 邵友濂 was appointed in the late Qing dynasty as the primary counselor (Toudeng canzan 头等参赞) to negotiate the return of the Yili 伊犁 region[1] conquered by Russia during the Dungan Revolt (Tongzhi huibian 同治回变),[2] and later the viceroy (Xunfu 巡抚) of Taiwan. His natural father Shao Heng 邵恒 was one of the most notorious dandies in Shanghai who squandered money and indulged in gambling. As Shao Yi 邵颐, the elder brother of Shao Heng, died young without an heir, Shao Youlian commanded in his last words that the eldest son of Shao Heng must be given to Mrs. Shi 史氏,[3] the widow of Shao Yi in order to maintain his lineage. Hence Shao Yunlong was adopted by Mrs. Shi and made the heir of the family.

The ethnicity of the family is rather unclear, as the systematic identification, classification and cartography of ethnic groups in China was done much later by the Communist government during 1949-1979. Regarding the family's ancestry, Shao's daughter Shao Xiaohong 邵绡红 writes: "On the mantelshelf in our living room there is a glass cabinet covered with silk. I heard that what's in it is the Family Tree of Shao. I've never seen it open. It gave me a sense of mystery. Then decades passed, and the glass cabinet has long disappeared." ("我家客厅壁炉架上有一只蒙了绸布的玻璃柜，听说里面摆的是《邵氏宗谱》。我从没见打开过，它给我一种神秘感。后来，风风雨雨几十年，那玻璃柜也不知去向了。")[4] She recalls that Shao once told her: "Our ancestor Shao Kangjie was Arabian. Because of his notable deeds, the emperor awarded him the name Shao. In Yuyao, our ancestral hall has a stele with Arabic on it." ("我们的祖先邵

---

[1] The majority of this region has become at the present day Yili Kazakh Autonomous Prefecture (Yili Hasake zizhizhou 伊犁哈萨克自治州).
[2] An ethnic and religious war fought between Han and Muslim minorities in central and western China during 1862-1877.
[3] Her full name is unknown.
[4] Shao Xiaohong, *Tiansheng de shiren—wode baba Shao Xunmei* 天生的诗人—我的爸爸邵洵美 [A Natural Born Poet: My Father Shao Xunmei] (Shanghai: Shanghai shudian chubanshe, 2015), 2.

康节是阿拉伯人。因为他有功，皇帝赐他姓邵。在余姚我们祠堂里的碑有阿拉伯文。")[5] But she later claimed that this might be a joke he made.[6]

Shao was educated by private tutors before he attended Shanghai St. John's High School, which was affiliated with St. John's University founded by the Episcopal Church in 1879. It is unclear to what extent the teaching of Christianity was incorporated into the school's coursework. According to the three biographies of Shao,[7] he never explicitly identified himself as a Christian and his religious views seem rather ambiguous. But it is clear that he is not unfamiliar with Christian texts, symbols and rituals. And as St John's taught most courses in English, it laid a solid foundation for his future acquaintance with Anglophone poetry.

Later Shao transferred to *Nanyang lukuang xuexiao* 南洋路矿学校, which was affiliated with *Nanyang gongxue* 南洋公学, a university founded by the famous industrialist Sheng Xuanhuai 盛宣怀.[8] As a family arrangement, Shao got engaged to Sheng's granddaughter Sheng Peiyu 盛佩玉 at the age of 17. This was a typical example of the alliance of ex-Qing officials and thriving industrial tycoons in the Republic of China. According to *My Father Shao Xunmei*, Shao changed his given name from Yunlong to Xunmei as he found out the name of his fiancée Peiyu 佩玉 (which can be literally translated as "adorned jade") appears in a poem entitled "Songs of Zheng·There is a Woman in the Carriage" (Zhengfeng·younü tongche 郑风·有女同车) from the *Book of Songs* (Shijing 诗经).[9] Hence he chose from the poem a juxtaposing term to be his name: Xunmei 洵美, which means in the context "indeed beautiful". However, a man changing

---

[5] Ibid., 441.

[6] Ibid., 443. The validity of her claim is in need of further examination.

[7] Besides *My Father Shao Xunmei*, 1) Sheng Peiyu 盛佩玉, *Shengshi jiazu: Shao Xunmei yu wo* 盛氏家族：邵洵美与我 [The Clan of Sheng: Shao Xunmei and Me] (Beijing: Renmin wenxue chubanshe, 2012) and 2) Lin Qi 林淇, *Haishang caizi—Shao Xunmei zhuan* 海上才子—邵洵美传) [Genius on the Sea: A Biography of Shao Xunmei] (Shanghai: Shanghai rennin wenxue chubanshe, 2002).

[8] Sheng Xuanhuai (1844-1916) was a businessman and statesman. He was a renowned figure in the Self-Strengthening Movement (Yangwu yundong 洋务运动), a movement from 1861 to 1895 supported by Qing government to learn Western technologies to help industrialize and modernize China.

[9] The sentence with Peiyu's name is "佩玉锵锵，洵美且都" (Peiyu qiangqiang, xunmei qiedu), which can be translated as "clanging adorned jade, indeed beautiful and refined". Ibid., 21-22. The *Book of Songs*, also translated as the *Classic of Poetry*, is the oldest collection of Chinese poetry. It includes 311 poems from the eleventh to the sixth century before Christ. The authors of these poems are unknown.

Introduction xiii

his given name for his fiancée is not a common practice in China. It could be a romantic, spontaneous idea of Shao, as *My Father Shao Xunmei* suggests. Or it could be a calculated action with an intent of flattery, as the family of Shao was losing its prestige while that of Sheng reached its vertex. Whichever way it is, the coalition of the two families provided Shao with an economic freedom most literati at the time could not obtain, while it also planted a mine for some left-wing attacks in the future.

In 1924 Shao went to Cambridge to study economics, but he soon found out his zest lay in literature. He made some bold attempts at translating and writing poetry, which will be dealt with at length in the first chapter of this book. In 1925 Shao visited Paris for the first time and happened to meet Xu Zhimo 徐志摩,[10] the cornerstone of the Crescent Moon Society (Xinyue she 新月社)[11] which had just become famous. In 1926 Shao left for Paris during the university vacation and enrolled as a part-time student at the École des Beaux-Arts.[12] During his stay, he met Xu Beihong 徐悲鸿,[13] the yet-to-be painter who then

---

[10] Xu Zhimo (1897-1931) was one of the most famous Chinese poets of the early twentieth century. He was educated in Beijing University, Clark University and the University of Cambridge. He attended Cambridge from 1921 to 1922, and therefore Shao did not get to meet him in England. Xu's most critically-acclaimed works include the poetry collections *Zhimo's Poems* (Zhimo de shi 志摩的诗) (1924) and *A Night in Florence* (Feilengcui de yiye 翡冷翠的一夜) (1927). At the age of 34, he died in an airplane crash amid gossips of a love triangle between him, his second wife Lu Xiaoman 陆小曼 and Lin Huiyin 林徽因, an architect and writer who was also married. Apart from that, his relationship with Pearl S. Buck is sometimes under vague suspicion for the interest of gossip. Xu is also loosely associated with the Bloomsbury Group for his attachment to Roger Fry and G. L. Dickinson.

[11] The Crescent Moon Society is an influential literary society founded by Xu Zhimo in 1923, named after "The Crescent Moon", a poem by Rabindranath Tagore. Other members of the society include Hu Shi 胡适, Liang Shiqiu 梁实秋, Shen Congwen 沈从文, Wen Yiduo 闻一多, Chen Mengjia 陈梦家 and Pan Guangdan 潘光旦. Some of these authors, such as Xu and Liang, are also considered a part of the Crescent Moon group (Xinyue pai 新月派), a school of poetry that is generally in favor of "art for art's sake". They used the newspaper *Supplements to Morning News* (Chenbao fukan 晨报副刊), and the journals *Crescent Moon* (Xinyue 新月) and *Poetry* (Shikan 诗刊) as the platforms for their views, mostly on arts and sometimes also on politics. It ceased operation in 1933.

[12] Heinrich Fruehauf, *Urban Exoticism in Modern Chinese Literature, 1910-1933* (Diss. University of Chicago, 1990), 230.

[13] Xu Beihong (1895-1953) was one of the most famous Chinese painters in the twentieth century, who is known for his Chinese ink paintings. He was educated in the École Nationale Supérieure des Beaux-Arts.

acquainted him with the Celestial Dog Club (Tiangou hui 天狗会),[14] a loosely formed arts society with the group of Zhang Daofan 张道藩,[15] Liu Jiwen 刘纪文,[16] Sun Peicang 孙佩苍,[17] Guo Youshou 郭有守[18] and Xie Shoukang 谢寿康[19]. The name of the club draws inspiration from the ancient Greek Cynics and the members were mostly Paris-based Chinese students. They frequented the cultural scenes of Paris such as the relocated Le Chat Noir[20] on Boulevard de Clichy and were interested in bringing cabaret culture to China.[21] The acquaintance with Xu Beihong and the Celestial Dog Club deepened Shao's understanding of literature and its cultural underpinning. Life in Paris also provided him with some training in French, though it could be deduced from the biographies that his acquisition of French never reached the same level as his English.

Later in 1926, Shao was informed of fire damage to one of his important family properties. He was forced to drop out of Cambridge and return to Shanghai to cope with the family business. On Shao's way back from England to Shanghai, he stayed at Singapore briefly and came across a literary journal called *New Epoch* (Xinjiyuan 新纪元), created by a group of Shanghai-based writers under the name of the Sphinx Club (Shihou she 狮吼社):[22] Teng Gu 腾固,[23]

---

[14] The name of the Celestial Dog Club also satirizes the Celestial Horse Club (Tianma hui 天马会), a society of painters formed in 1919. The latter includes members such as Jiang Xiaojian 江小鹣, Ding Song 丁悚 and Wang Yachen 汪亚尘.

[15] Zhang Daofan (1897-1968) was a politician and art critic. He was educated in the University of London and the École Nationale Supérieure des Beaux-Arts.

[16] Liu Jiwen (1890-1957) was a statesman. He was educated in The London School of Economics and Political Science.

[17] Sun Peicang (1890-1942) was a statesman who was educated in the École des Beaux-Arts.

[18] Guo Youshou (1901-1977) was a statesman educated in Université de Paris.

[19] Xie Shoukang (1897-1974) was a literary critic. He was educated in Université Libre de Bruxelles and L'École Libre des Sciences Politiques.

[20] Le Chat Noir was a famous cabaret in Paris whose patrons include Paul Verlaine and Claude Debussy. Its first site opened from 1881 to 1897. Its last site opened in 1907 and was popular in the 20s.

[21] Ibid., 100-101.

[22] The Sphinx Club started in July 1924 when *Sphinx Fortnightly* (Shihou banyuekan 狮吼半月刊) was launched. The club ended in September 1930, when *La Maison D'Or Monthly* (Jinwu yuekan 金屋月刊) ceased publication.

[23] Teng Gu (1901-1941) was a writer and literary critic. He was educated in Universität zu Berlin. His critically-acclaimed works include two collections of short novels entitled *Murals* (Bihua 壁画) (1924) and *Extra-marital* (Waiyu 外遇) (1928).

Zhang Kebiao 章克标[24] and Fang Guangdao 方光焘.[25] This journal had a hunger for Baudelaire, Verlaine and Wilde, which is in line with Shao's personal taste. After he came back to Shanghai, he managed to meet Teng and gradually became acquainted with the Sphinx Club. Some of his earliest works were published in *Tusu* (屠苏), another journal edited by the Sphinx Club after *New Epoch* ceased publication. As Teng soon proceeded to pursue a political career and *Tusu* closed down, Shao took over the role of editor-in-chief and wielded his financial capability to support the publication of three journals: *Sphinx Monthly* (Shihou yuekan 狮吼月刊) from May 1927 to March 1928, *Sphinx Fortnightly* (Shihou banyuekan 狮吼半月刊) from July 1928 to December 1928, and *La Maison D'Or Monthly* (Jinwu yuekan 金屋月刊) from Jan 1929 to Sep 1930. These journals mainly feature poetry and prose contributed by writers associated with the Sphinx Club, as well as translated poems and short stories. These journals served as a platform for Shao's experiments in poetics and literary translation, which led to his publication of *Fire and Flesh* (Huo yu rou 火与肉), an anthology of critical essays in 1928.[26] In the same year, he published *Roses and Roses* (Yiduoduo meigui 一朵朵玫瑰), a collection of translated poems.[27] In 1927 Shao published his first poetry collection *Heaven and May*

---

[24] Zhang Kebiao (1900-2007) was a writer and publisher. He was educated in Kyoto Imperial University. He helped establish Times Publishing House (Shidai tushu gongsi 时代图书公司), one of the biggest publishers in the 30s.

[25] Fang Guangtao (1898-1964) was a linguist and writer. He was educated in Université de Lyon. His famous works include linguistic essays "System and Method" (Tixi yu fangfa 体系与方法) (1939) and "Does discourse have class?" (Yanyu you jiejixing ma 言语有阶级性吗?) (1959).

[26] In the dedication Shao cites "Hands that sting like fire" from Swinburne's "Before Dawn", which might be the inspiration for the title *Fire and Flesh*. The anthology includes "Gautier" (Gaodiai 高谛蔼), which Shao describes as his translation of an essay of Arthur Symons on Gautier (the source text is unknown), and five essays written by Shao: "Sappho" (Shafu 莎茀) which talks about Sappho; "Catullus's Love poems" (Jiaduoluosi de qingshi 迦多罗斯的情诗) that dwells on Gaius Valerius Catullus (c. 84 - c. 54 BC), a poet of the late Roman Republic; "Swinburne" (Shiwenpeng 史文朋) and "Songs before Sunrise" (Richuqian zhi ge 日出前之歌) that pivot on Swinburne; as well as "A Sort of Cross Between a Thieves' Kitchen and a Presbytery" (Zeiku yu shengmiao zhijian de xintu 贼窟与圣庙之间的信徒) which focuses on Verlaine and the title of which comes from chapter VII of Moore's *Memoirs of My Dead Life*. In the foreword of the anthology Shao also mentions he is drafting an essay on Baudelaire, which he hopes could be included in a future reprint. It seems that it never happened.

[27] The anthology includes translations of poems written by Sappho, Catullus, Verlaine, Gautier, Dante and Christina Rossetti, Swinburne, Hardy and Sara Teasdale.

(Tiantang yu wuyue 天堂与五月), and in the next year came the second collection *Flower-like Evil* (Huayiban de zui'e 花一般的罪恶). After this, his focus shifted to poetry criticism and it was not until 1936 that his third collection *Twenty-five Poems*[28] (Shi ershiwushou 诗二十五首) was published.

Shao and Sheng Peiyu officially got married in 1927. In 1935 Shao got acquainted with Emily Hahn, an American columnist living in Shanghai. According to the biography *Emily Hahn in Shanghai* (Xiangmeili zai Shanghai 项美丽在上海),[29] their friendship soon morphed into an affair. This relationship was approved by Sheng as she regarded Hahn merely as a concubine he kept. After the Japanese army conquered Shanghai in 1937, Hahn and Shao's family moved to Avenue Joffre in the French Concession. The relationship eventually came to a halt in 1939. Hahn left Shanghai and their correspondence was cut off by the war. It was not until 1945 that they managed to exchange letters again.

Shao lost many of his book stores and publishing houses in the Japanese-conquered Shanghai. After the Communist Party came to power in 1949, his family wealth shrank drastically. He stopped writing poetry and tried to make a living by translating Anglophone literature, such as Shelley's *Prometheus Unbound*, *Queen Mab*, Byron's *The Age of Bronze* and Gaskell's *Mary Barton* (co-translated with She Guitang 佘贵堂). In 1958 Shao was put in prison accused of being an imperialist spy. Wang Pu writes that what triggered his imprisonment might be that Shao wrote a letter to Hahn, who was then back in America, and tried to borrow money for his sixth brother Shao Yunxiang 邵云骧, who was poverty-stricken in Hong Kong. The letter never got out of China for it was intercepted by the police.[30] In 1962 Shao was released, but being impoverished, he again tried to ask Hahn for help in 1966, the year when the Cultural Revolution began. Although he submitted a copy to the police in advance and stated the purpose of the letter, still it could not be delivered.[31] Two years later, he died in poverty.

However, Shao's correspondence with Hahn might not be the only reason that led to his interrogation and imprisonment. In the 1920s, Shao had a few

---

[28] The title bears a resemblance to Tristan Tzara's poetry collection *Vingt-cinq poèmes* in 1918. However, Shao never mentions Tzara in his works and it is unclear whether this is simply a coincidence.
[29] Wang Pu 王璞, *Xiangmeili zai Shanghai* 项美丽在上海 [Emily Hahn in Shanghai] (Beijing: Renmin wenxue chubanshe, 2005).
[30] Ibid., 292.
[31] Ibid., 292.

disputes with left-wing writers. His publications instigated a profusion of ironic attacks from Lu Xun 鲁迅,[32] probably the most studied modern Chinese writer:

> Mr. Shao Xunmei is a so-called "poet",[33] and the grandson-in-law of the famous tycoon "Sheng Gongbao".[34] If one wants to splash foul water on the head of "such a person", it's quite understandable. But I do think being a writer is ultimately different from arranging "an extravagant funeral procession". Even if the writer hires a huge flock of supporters who pave the way with gongs and drums to boost his works, it's still an empty street afterwards. But for "an extravagant funeral procession", after several decades there'll still be folks talking about it. If extremely poor, one certainly can't write. But gold and silver are not the seeds of literature either and so it would be better to use the money to buy some land along the Yangtze River. Yet a rich fellow sometimes gets this wrong and thinks that since money makes the world go round, then it can also make him a good writer. Money makes the world go round, maybe even the universe, but it won't make you a good writer, and the poetry of the poet Shao Xunmei demonstrates this.

> 邵洵美先生是所谓 "诗人"，又是有名的巨富 "盛宫保" 的孙婿，将污秽泼在 "这般东西" 的头上，原也十分平常的。但我以为作文人究竟和 "大出丧" 有些不同，即使雇得一大群帮闲，开锣喝道，过后仍是一条空街，还不及 "大出丧" 的虽在数十年后，有时还有几个市侩传颂。穷极，文是不能工的，可是金银又并非文章的根苗，它最好还是买长江沿岸的田地。然而富家儿总不免常常误解，以为钱可使鬼，就也可以通文。使鬼，

---

[32] Lu Xun (1881-1936) was an influential writer and literary critic. He studied medicine in Japan but eventually turned to literature. His most famous works include collections of short stories *Call to Arms* (Nahan 呐喊) (1923), *Wandering* (Panghuang 彷徨) (1926) and *A Brief History of Chinese Fiction* (Zhongguo xiaoshuo shilue 中国小说史略) (1923). He helped found the League of Left-wing Writers (Zhongguo zuoyi zuojia lianmeng 中国左翼作家联盟), often abbreviated as Left League (Zuolian 左联), which was formed in 1930 with the aid of the Communist Party. Other important members include Mao Dun 茅盾, Guo Moruo 郭沫若 and Ding Ling 丁玲. The purpose of the League was to advance the development of proletarian literature.

[33] Here Lu Xun uses inverted commas to quote phrases from Shao's article "Literati Have No Jobs" (Wenren wuhang 文人无行) in the second issue of the journal *Conversations of Ten Days* (Shiri tan 十日谈), published in August 1933.

[34] Sheng Gongbao 盛宫保 is an honorable title of Sheng Xuanhuai.

大概是确的，也许还可以通神，但通文却不成，诗人邵洵美先生本身的诗便是证据。35

The taunts of Lu Xun evolved in their degree of nastiness as Shao, in 1929, became closely associated with the Crescent Moon Society, the major foe of the left-wing literati grouped around Lu Xun. He remarks: "Because of his forefathers' credits he got a huge mansion; so we don't need to ask whether he got it through frauds, robberies, legal inheritance, or the trade-off for being the son-in-law." ("因为祖上的阴功，得了一所大宅子，且不问他是骗来的，抢来的，或合法继承，或是做了女婿换来的。")36 In the footnote of this sentence, he says: "The people being mocked here are those who became rich sons-in-law and flaunted their wealth, like Shao Xunmei." ("这里讽刺的是做了富家翁的女婿而炫耀于人的邵洵美之流。")37 As Lu Xun is the most influential left-wing literary critic and the flagman of the left-wing literature upheld by the Communist Party, his verdict on Shao persisted in rendering Shao's works under-evaluated and even subject to political interrogation after 1949.

Besides Lu Xun's venomous verdict, Leo Lee ascribes the long-time marginalization of Shao to the perception that "he was the least suited to the May Fourth prototype of a writer of social conscience".38 Social conscience, especially a social conscience in the format of a left-wing writer was what literary criticism emphasized in the post-1949 period. Wu Zhongjie 吴中杰 writes:

> After 1949 the research of literary history usually divides writers into groups according to their political views, especially the research on the history of Republican literature. Take the literature of the 30s as an example: left-wing literature sets the standard and is the focus of the research; other schools are generally marginalized, and the arts that stand directly opposite to the left-wing get nothing except a few lines of political criticism.

---

35 Lu Xun, "Houji" 后记 [Afterword], in *Zhunfengyue tan* 准风月谈 [On Demimonde] (Beijing: Renmin wenxue chubanshe, 2006), 188.
36 Lu, *Complete Works of Lu Xun*, 6:40.
37 Ibid.
38 Leo Lee, *Shanghai Modern: The Flowering of a New Urban Culture in China* (Cambridge, Mass.; London: Harvard University Press, 1999), 241.

建国以后的文学史研究，大抵以作家的政治态度为分野，现代文学史研究尤其如此。以 20 世纪 30 年代的文学为例，左翼文学是坐标轴，也是研究的重点，别的派别则渐远渐疏，到得与左翼对立的文艺，则除了几句政治批判的语言之外，就没有什么内容了。[39]

Even though Shao did have friction with the left-wing literati in the 30s, I would venture to say his social conscience was certainly not non-existent and his political ground does not stand "directly opposite" to the left wing. When Xia Yan 夏衍,[40] the forerunner of the left-wing film movement was stuck in financial problems in 1928, Shao assisted him in publishing his works and paid him in advance. In 1931, after Hu Yepin 胡也频,[41] a communist writer, was executed by the Kuomintang and Shen Congwen 沈从文[42] escorted Hu's wife Ding Ling 丁玲[43] and children back to Hunan, Shao provided them with financial help. During the Sino-Japanese War Shao and Hahn launched *Pool of Freedom* (Ziyoutan 自由潭), a political journal that promoted resistance to the Japanese army in the besieged Shanghai. He even helped translate Mao Zedong's "On Protracted War" (Lun chijiuzhan 论持久战) into English, circulated the translation in Shanghai and published it serially in *Candid Comment* (Zhiyan pinglun 直言评论), an English journal that he co-edited with

---

[39] Wu Zhongjie 吴中杰, "Xu" 序 [Preface], in *Yigeren de tanhua* 一个人的谈话 [Conversations of One Man] (Shanghai: Shanghai shudian chubanshe, 2012), 1. "Conversations of One Man" was originally a column Shao started in *Human Words Weekly* (Renyan zhoukan 人言周刊) in 1934. In 2012 it was included along with some other works in the anthology *Conversations of One Man*.

[40] Xia Yan (1900-1995) was a playwright and art critic. He was educated in Kyushu Imperial University. His famous works include film scripts *Raging Waves* (Kuangliu 狂流) (1933) and *Children of Trouble Time* (Fengyun ernü 风云儿女) (1935).

[41] Hu Yepin (1903-1931) was a writer and social activist. He is considered one of the Five Martyrs of the Left League as he was arrested and executed by the Kuomintang for attending a secret Communist Party meeting in Shanghai. The other four are Rou Shi 柔石, Yin Fu 殷夫, Li Weisen 李伟森 and Feng Keng 冯铿.

[42] Shen Congwen (1902-1988) was a writer and art critic. He was most famous for novels and short stories based on the regional culture and his life experiences in west Hunan. His most critically-acclaimed works include the novel *Border Town* (Biancheng 边城) (1934) and *A Study on Chinese Ancient Clothing* (Zhongguo gudai fushi yanjiu 中国古代服饰研究) (1981).

[43] Ding Ling (1904-1986) was a writer and social activist. She was educated in Shanghai University. Her critically-acclaimed works include novels *Miss Sophie's Diary* (Shafei nüshi de riji 莎菲女士的日记) (1930) and *The Sun Shines over the Sanggan River* (Taiyang zhaozai Sangganhe shang 太阳照在桑干河上) (1948).

Hahn in the Shanghai French Concession, which was then a bold and courageous move.[44] After the war, his publishing house also supported the publications of many Marxist works, though most of them are associated with Trotsky and the Second International, hence drawing negative criticism after 1949.

The charge against Shao as an imperialist spy was revoked posthumously in 1985. But even after 1985, little research was done until several volumes of his collected works were published after 2006, hence making his textual corpus visible again to critical attention. Scholars such as Li Guangde 李广德, Chen Zishan 陈子善, Wang Jingfang 王京芳, Hal Swindall and Jonathan Hutt have paved the way and filled the vacuum bit by bit.

Shao is a practitioner of New Poetry (Xinshi 新诗). The term New Poetry in its Chinese socio-historical context refers to the poetry that is written in the vernacular language rather than classical Chinese and that does not conform to the forms of classical Chinese poetry. New Poetry sprouted with the New Culture Movement (Xinwenhua yundong 新文化运动)[45] and the May Fourth Movement (Wusi yundong 五四运动).[46] It can be conceived as a resistance, or a remedy to the stagnation with which classical Chinese poetry was confronted in the late Qing dynasty. And as the "new poets" endeavor to free themselves from the stagnant confinement of classical Chinese poetry, they often actively assimilate the influence of foreign poetry and wield it to break the shackles that have constrained their creativity. In this regard, it would be unwise to forgo a discussion about the influence of foreign poetry on the formation of Chinese New Poetry.

Although New Poetry is often associated with the New Culture and May Fourth Movement, it does not mean that there were no attempts at reforming the Chinese poetry in the decades that lead up to the 1910s. In the 1890s, poets associated with the Hundred Days' Reform Movement (Wuxu bianfa 戊戌变

---

[44] Ibid., 2.

[45] The New Culture Movement refers to a series of events in 1910s and 1920s that calls for the use of vernacular language in literature, the re-examination of Confucianism and any norms, ideas that are associated with the feudal past of China. The movement was led by wrtiers Hu Shi 胡适, Lu Xun 鲁迅, Li Dazhao 李大钊, Chen Duxiu 陈独秀 and Qian Xuantong 钱玄同.

[46] The May Fourth Movement denotes the student protests on 4 May 1919 against the Chinese government's concession that allowed Japan to take over the German colonies in Shandong as a part of the Treaty of Versailles. In a broader sense it also refers to the political ramifications of these protests in the 1920s, and can be seen as a part of the New Culture Movement.

法),[47] such as Liang Qichao 梁启超[48] and Huang Zunxian 黄遵宪,[49] engaged in practices of poetic inventions and theoretical exploration. The dictum for their attempts can be summarized by a line from a poem of Huang entitled "Assorted Feelings" (Zagan 杂感): "My hands write my mouth." ("我手写我口")[50] However, though they stress the importance of using vernacular language in poetic practices, they do not succeed in breaking the formal restraints of classical Chinese poetry. Their primary focus, just like the dilemma existing in their political agendas, is a reform which, in its nature, only allows a certain amount of changes that cannot fundamentally change the reformed entity. The failure of the reformist poets denotes that Chinese poetry at its creative plateau could not achieve a thorough transformation in language and form simply through an internal reform rushed in a short time. At a time when cultural exchanges between China and the West became increasingly frequent, assimilating the influence of foreign, especially Western poetry in order to advance the stagnated Chinese poetry seemed to have its historical rationality.

Hu Shi 胡适,[51] who is often considered the forerunner of New Poetry, was influenced by Darwin's theory of evolution when he studied in America. He attempted to write vernacular poetry not conforming to the forms of classical Chinese poetry, as he believed the classical Chinese poetry did not fit the new material and phenomena in a swiftly changing world. In the preface to the reprint of *A Collection of Attempts* he describes "Cannot Be Confined" (Guanbuzhu le 关不住了), his translation of Sara Teasdale's[52] "Over the Roofs",

---

[47] The Hundred Days' Reform is an unsuccessful reform in 1898 that lasted for only 104 days. One of the most important agendas of this reform was to change the Qing government from absolute monarchy to constitutional monarchy.
[48] Liang Qichao (1873-1929) was an influential writer, historian and politician who became one of the major proponents of the Hundred Days' Reform.
[49] Huang Zunxian (1848-1905) was a poet, diplomat and a participant of the Hundred Days' Reform.
[50] Huang, *Huang Zunxian shi xuan* 黄遵宪诗选 [An Anthology of Huang Zunxian] (Beijing: Zhonghua shuju, 2008), 8.
[51] Hu Shi (1891-1962) was a writer, philosopher and one of the central figures in the New Culture Movement. He was educated in Cornell and Columbia University. His most critically-acclaimed works include *A Survey of the History of Chinese Philosophy* (Zhongguo zhexueshi dagang 中国哲学史大纲) (1919) and *A Collection of Attempts* (Changshiji 尝试集) (1920), the first vernacular poetry collection during the New Culture Movement.
[52] Sara Teasdale (1884-1933) was an American poet. Her famous works include the poetry collections *Love Songs* (1917) and *Flame and Shadow* (1920).

as "the founding epoch" ("成立的纪元") of his New Poetry.[53] In the article "A Preliminary Discussion of Literature Reform" (Wenxue gailiang chuyi 文学改良刍议, 1917) he enunciates eight guidelines on what to avoid when writing new literature,[54] which bear much similarity to Ezra Pound's "A Few Don'ts by an Imagiste" in *Poetry* March 1913 issue, as well as the six rules given in the preface to the anthology *Some Imagist Poets* edited by Amy Lowell[55] in 1916.

The influence of foreign poetry can also be seen in other "new poets". Xu Zhimo, Wenyi Duo 闻一多[56] were influenced by the Victorians and British early modernists, while Li Jinfa 李金发[57] and Dai Wangshu 戴望舒[58] drew inspiration from the French symbolists. Bing Xin's 冰心[59] and Zong Baihua's 宗白华[60]

---

[53] Hu, *Changshiji* 尝试集 [A Collection of Attempts] (Beijing: Beijing renmin wenxue chubanshe, 2000), 183.

[54] Published in *New Youth* (Xinqingnian 新青年) volum 2, issue 5 (1917). *New Youth* is an influential magazine during the New Culture Movement. Launched in 1915, it was edited in turn by Chen Duxiu 陈独秀, Qian Xuantong 钱玄同, Hu Shi 胡适, Li Dazhao 李大钊, Liu Bannong 刘半农 and Lu Xun 鲁迅. It ceased publication in 1926.

[55] Amy Lowell (1874-1925) was an American imagist poet. Her famous works include poetry collections *A Dome of Many-Coloured Glass* (1912) and *Sword Blades and Poppy Seed* (1914).

[56] Wen Yiduo (1899-1946) was a poet and art critic. He was educated in Tsinghua University and School of the Art Institute of Chicago. His poetry collections *Red Candle* (Hongzhu 红烛) (1923) and *Dead Pool* (Sishui 死水) (1928) are particularly famous.

[57] Li Jinfa (1900-1976) was a poet and art critic who is often considered as a Chinese symbolist. Educated in École nationale supérieure des beaux-arts, he is famous for his poetry collections *A Little Rain* (Weiyu 微雨) (1925) and *Sing for Happiness* (Wei xingfu erge 为幸福而歌) (1926).

[58] Dai Wangshu (1905-1950) was a poet and translator who is regarded as a key figure in Chinese symbolism. He was educated in Fudan University and Université de Paris. His most famous work is the poetry collection *My Memories* (Wode jiyi 我的记忆) (1929).

[59] Bing Xin (1900-1999) was a translator, social activist and one of the most famous Chinese female writers in the twentieth century. She was educated in Yanjing University and Wellesley College in America, and taught in Tokyo University. Her most critically-acclaimed works include the short novel *Superman* (Chaoren 超人) (1920), the poetry collection *Stars and Spring Water* (Fanxing chunshui 繁星春水) (1923) and a collection of causeries entitled *To Young Readers* (Ji xiaoduzhe 寄小读者) (1923), which is considered as the cornerstone for the children's literature in China.

[60] Zong Baihua (1897-1986) was a poet and art critic. He was educated in Universität Frankfurt am Main and Universität zu Berlin. His major works include an anthology of essays entitled *A Walk of Aesthetics* (Meixue sanbu 美学散步) (1987) and an anthology of essays and poetry entitled *The Realm of Arts* (Yijing 艺境) (1998).

Introduction xxiii

exploration of "small poems" (Xiaoshi 小诗)[61] shared the same interest with Zhou Zuoren's 周作人[62] translations of Japanese tankas[63] and haikus[64]. These poets all had the experience of studying abroad and they all obtained the proficiency of at least one foreign language. Their direct contact with the foreign, especially Western poetry, laid a foundation for the birth and development of Chinese New Poetry.

In a narrow sense, New Poetry is often conceived as a term that only refers to the poetic exploration made in the 1910s and 1920s. In a broader sense, the development of New Poetry can be summarized into three stages. The first stage is the 1910s to 1940s, when the New Culture Movement gradually became radical against the Chinese traditional culture, as many proponents regarded the medium of traditional culture, namely the classical Chinese and the literary forms composed of it, as outmoded and unfit for the modern jungle. When it comes to the realm of poetry, some extremists even attempted to eradicate the influence of classical Chinese poetry and its cultural underpinnings in order to make room for the new-born New Poetry. The second phase is the 1950s to 1970s, when poetry, and writing poetry, had complicated political ramifications. The artistic concerns of New Poetry were no longer important at this stage, as political-correctness became the primary issue. The last period is from the 1980s till now, when New Poetry seems to have detached from what its name once denoted. For the poetry practitioners who have been writing in vernacular language and reading a profusion of canonized New Poetry for decades, the idea of New Poetry has long lost its newness. It has been there too long and nowadays it is difficult not to conceive it as a dominating norm, or shackle, of writing poetry. In order to get rid of this new shackle and pursue the further possibilities of poetry, it is beneficial to look back at the time when New Poetry

---

[61] Xiaoshi usually refers to poems whose length is but one to five lines. It appeared as a literary trend at about the same time as the May Fourth Movement, but gradually faded in mid 1920s. The fashion of Xiaoshi was influenced by the translations of Japanese short poems and the works of Rabindranath Tagore (1861-1941), an Indian poet and social activist.

[62] Zhou Zuoren (1885-1967) was a writer and translator, a brother of Lu Xun (whose original name is Zhou Shuren 周树人). He studied in Japan at Hosei University and Rikkyo University. He is a controversial figure as he once worked for the Japanese puppet government during the Sino-Japanese War, and was accused of treason after the war.

[63] In classical Japanese literature, waka 和歌 is a type of poems written in Japanese, which is contrasted to kanshi 汉诗, the poems written by Japanese poets in classical Chinese. Tanka 短歌, which can be translated as "short poem", is the most common type of waka with five lines and the syllabic pattern of 5-7-5-7-7.

[64] Haiku 俳句 refers to a type of Japanese poems with three lines and the syllabic pattern of 5-7-5.

was at its cradle, to understand how this norm was constructed in the very beginning, and survey the Western influences that were important to the shaping of New Poetry. Therefore, in this book, I chose Shao, one of the central figures for translating and introducing Western poetry into China, as an important node in the network of literary influence that connects China and the West.

0.2 Shao and Western poetry

The birth of New Poetry, in a broader context, is an important constituent of the New Culture Movement. New Poetry is the cause, and also the outcome of the revolution of literature that the New Culture Movement ardently proposes. The translation and circulation of foreign, especially Western poetry in China contributes tremendously to the formation of this New Culture. However, though Western poetry and theories serve as the catalyst to the transformation of Chinese poetry in the 1910s and 1920s, it is not to be understood that Chinese New Poetry is only shaped by the Western poetry introduced to the Chinese poetry practitioners in the period. The fundamental reason for the transformation still lies in the ontological crisis within the classical Chinese poetry, which became increasingly prominent at the turn of the century. The New Poetry is constructed through actively, purposefully assimilating the influence of classical Chinese poetry and foreign, especially Western poetry. In this way, it becomes something that is heterogeneous, or I should say "foreign", to both its classical ancestors and foreign poetry.

Shao's involvement with Western, especially Anglophone poetry, is often clearly enunciated in his works. *Heaven and May*, Shao's first poetry collection features a poem "Anch'io sono pittore!",[65] in which he arranges a fantastic gathering with his poetic idols:

> I dreamed of standing beside Poe's seat,
> Birds sing in the rosy ambiance,
> Sappho plucks her seven-stringed lyre;
> Swinburne holds his fiery love light;
> Keats wakes up hearing a nightingale,
> Regorged tears bitter the once sweet heart,

---

[65] The original title is in Italian, which means "I am also a painter". It is a phrase that is often bound with the story that Correggio made this exclamation after seeing a painting of Raphael, which might be either the *Sistine Madonna* now in the Gemäldegalerie Alte Meister in Dresden or the *Ecstasy of St. Cecilia* in La Pinacoteca Nacional de Bolonia. Some scholars think the story is untrue for Correggio did not have access to the two works.

He's a shepherd lying on the grass,
The moon sneaks in to steal a kiss;

我梦见立在爱普老的座旁,
玫瑰花的座周有小鸟歌唱,
莎弗拨弹着她七弦的仙琴;
史文朋抱着他火般的爱光;
济慈正睡醒了痴听着夜莺,
倒流的泪染苦了甜蜜的心,
他是个牧羊儿在草上横卧,
月娘战战兢兢地过来偷吻;⁶⁶

These poetic idols, with the exception of Sappho, are all Anglophone writers. In the preface to his third collection *Twenty-five Poems* published nine years later, Shao comments on his earlier experiments in imitating his poetic icons: "Traces of foreign poems permeate my lines. I used to imitate their patterns on purpose, but my attitude was not pedantic. By no means did I want to introduce a new shackle; I wanted to find a new order." ("外国诗的踪迹在我的字句里是随处可以寻得的。我也曾故意地去摹仿过他们的格律,但是我的态度不是迂腐的,我决不想介绍一个新桎梏,我是要发现一种新秩序。")⁶⁷ Shao states that he used to "imitate their patterns on purpose", which refers to his attempts to deploy the meters used in Western poetry to Chinese poetry. This denotes that Shao used to experiment on the metricalization of New Poetry. His experiments are different from the New Poetry that the New Culture Movement initially advocated, which uses almost exclusively free verse. Brian Skerratt writes:

> The New Poetry movement had begun by attacking the native classical tradition and its representative form, regulated verse (lüshi 律詩), which was caricatured as impossibly rigid and constraining in its prosodic

---

⁶⁶ Originally included in *Heaven and May*; here quoted from *Huayiban de zui'e: Shao Xunmei zuopin xilie shigejuan* 花一般的罪恶: 邵洵美作品系列 诗歌卷 [Flower-like Evil: Poetic Works of Shao Xunmei] (Shanghai: Shanghai shudian chubanshe, 2012), 122. As the anthology's title comes from Shao's second poetry collection *Flower-like Evil*, to avoid ambiguity my book will refer to the anthology as *Poetic Works of Shao Xunmei* hereafter.
⁶⁷ Shao Xunmei, "Shi ershiwushou zixu" 诗二十五首自序 [Preface to Twenty-five Poems], in *Xunmei wencun* 洵美文存 [Collected Works of Shao Xunmei], ed. Chen Zishan 陈子善 (Shenyang: Liaoning jiaoyu chubanshe, 2006), 365.

rules; free your verse, the thinking went, and individual freedom from the shackles of tradition would follow.[68]

At the beginning of the New Culture Movement, the adoption of free verse and the emancipation from the confinement of tradition seems to be equated, in an oversimplified way. When the New Culture Movement began, there was only a small amount of poets who attempted at metricalization. But the situation changed as the movement carried on into the mid-1920s. Li Changkong 李长空 observes: "When Chinese New Poetry was born, it was divided into free verse and metrical verse [...] Free verse took center stage while metrical New Poetry was at the ignored margin." ("中国新诗诞生之初，即分化为自由诗和格律体新诗两种形式 [...] 自由诗占据了主流地位，格律体新诗曾经一度处于被忽略的边沿位置。")[69] He states that the arbitrariness ("随意性") and uncertainty ("不确定性") of free verse "became a critical problem and hindrance to its own development, which makes it difficult for the poetry critics and practitioners to construct an aesthetic standard of free verse or achieve a consensus on its aesthetics." ("成为其发展的严重弊端和障碍，使得诗歌界一直难以构建其审美规范，更无法达成其审美共识。")[70] Mao Han 毛翰 upholds this observation:

> Ever since Chinese New Poetry (vernacular verse, free verse) was born, the validity of its art, the necessity of its existence, had always been questioned. New Poetry itself sometimes also lacks confidence or even abases itself, when it comes to the vernacular language and the formal aspect of free verse. In this regard, a reconstruction of the metrics was proposed and metricalization seems to be a dose of effective medicine to cure New Poetry.
>
> 中国新诗 (白话诗、自由诗) 问世以来，其艺术的合法性，存在的必要性，一直受到质疑。 新诗自己对于这种白话的语言风格，自由的形式特征，

---

[68] Brian Skerratt, "Reading Modernity Musically: Zhu Guangqian and the Rhythm of New Poetry", *Chinese Literature: Essays, Articles, Reviews* 2015, vol. 37: 113.
[69] Li Changkong, "Gelüti xinshi xingshi yu neirong de tongyi" 格律体新诗形式与内容的统一 [Unity of Form and Content in Chinese New Metrical Poetry], *Jiangsu daxue xuebao (shehuikexueban)* 江苏大学学报 (社会科学版) [Journal of Jiangsu University (Social Science Edition)] 2010, no. 2: 55.
[70] Ibid.

有时也缺乏信心，乃至自相菲薄。于是，重建诗的格律被提了出来，格律化似乎成为救治新诗的一剂良方。[71]

One of the pioneers who put forth such a proposal is Wen Yiduo, whom I have briefly mentioned in the previous section. He proposes that New Poetry should have "musical beauty" ("音乐的美"), which could be achieved by the creation of a system of metrics that does not exist in the classical Chinese poetry.[72] Skerratt considers this a reaction "against the vogue for prose-like free verse and advocating the use of regular meters on the model of European poetry."[73] Wen's proposal resonates with many experiments of his contemporary poets, as well as their discussions on the effect brought by the introduction of European meters into Chinese. These contemporary poets include Shao. On one occasion, he makes a comparison of the benefits and drawbacks of pentameter and tetrameter:

> For example, the forte of pentameter is that it can extend the power of concentration; it can have more natural and complicated variations. It has intermissions, but the style is coherent. Even if the reader takes a rest whilst reading or puts it aside for a few days, his spirit can still concentrate when he picks it back up [...] Tetrameter has fewer variations. It can get boring when written long, but its temperament is more amiable, simpler and suitable for innocent situations [...] I think a true poet must have his own "best order". A fixed meter wouldn't help him, nor would it get in his way. So rather than saying that meter is a standard for people who write poems, we should say it's more of a direction for people who read poems. The permutation of words and the arrangement of sounds are just for the convenience of others' appreciation.

> 譬如"五步无韵诗"的特点是在能使清境的力量延长，它可以有更自然更复杂的变化；它也有间断，但气韵是连贯的，读的人即使在中间休息一下，甚至搁置几天，但是当他要继续读下去的时候，精神仍旧能会聚 [...] "四

---

[71] Mao Han, "Xinshi gelühua de santiao kexing zhi lu" 新诗格律化的三条可行之路 [Three Possible Ways for the Metricalization of New Poetry], *Dongnan xueshu* 东南学术 [Southeast Academic Research] 2014, no. 1: 223.

[72] Wen Yiduo, "Shi de gelü" 诗的格律 [The Metrics of Poetry], *Wen yiduo quanji, di er juan* 闻一多全集，第 2 卷 [Complete Works of Wen Yiduo, vol. 2]. Beijing: Hubei renmin chubanshe (1993), 137. Originally published in *Morning Post · Poetry* (Chenbao shijuan 晨报·诗镌), 13 May 1926.

[73] Skerratt, 113.

步无韵诗"变化的可能少，太长了会单调，但是它的情致更来得亲切，更来得素朴，适宜于更天真的意境 [...] 我觉得一个真正的诗人一定有他自己的"最好的秩序"。固定的格律不会给他帮助，也不会给他妨碍。所以我们与其说格律是给写诗人的一种规范，不如说是给读诗人的一种指点，字句的排列与音韵的布置，不过是为便利别人去欣赏。[74]

It should be brought to our attention that in the vernacular language which the New Culture Movement ardently advocates, the proportion of two- and three-character words greatly increased, as compared to the dominance of one-character words in the classical Chinese. As each Chinese character is mono-syllabic, the increase of two- and three-character words means that there emerged many new and yet confusing possibilities to talk about rhythm and what rhythm can signify in the poetry written in this new language. Besides, the drastic change of social and economic circumstances yielded a profusion of words coming from heterogeneous cultural sources. Many poets including Shao were struggling to explore how New Poetry could be "poetic" from the chasm of the old poetics and the new language material, not to mention many radical voices that suggested not just the simplification of how Chinese is written but the complete romanization of the Chinese language.

Shao holds that though New Poetry abolishes the patterns used in classical Chinese poetry, it does not necessarily mean that New Poetry cannot try out new patterns. In this sense the newness of New Poetry lies not only in the defiance of conventions of classical Chinese poetry, but also the attempts of putting this new Chinese language into chains that have been well-wrought in a heterogeneous language and watching it dance, gracefully or wonkily.

As Shao maintains in the above-cited excerpts that "By no means did I want to introduce a new shackle; I was to find a new order" and that "a true poet must have his own 'best order'", the attempts of finding the best order for him involves the formal influence of Western poetry. Out of all the daring experiments, "Sappho" (Shafu 莎茀), Shao's rendering of sapphics, is a good example. The borrowing of the form of sapphics is an act of investigation into the possibilities of rhythm when the new Chinese language in the making is stuffed into a form that relies on quantitative meter. The problem thus engendered is that there is no differentiation of syllable weight in Chinese, either the classical or this new-born baby. There is simply no essential stress variation in Chinese. In this regard, the only thing that can remain seems to be just the transplantation of the 11/11/11/5 stanza scheme. But to Shao, the extent of successfully adapting the actual form of sapphics gradually becomes

---

[74] Shao, "Preface to *Twenty-five Poems*", *Collected Works of Shao Xunmei*, 369.

not that important when compared to the migration of the idea of Sappho. To him, Sappho is an embodiment of poetry and its possibilities, which I will discuss in the first chapter. It is the empty body of Sappho that is yearning for the filling of new flesh in each occasion of resurrection. These occasions are the very moments when a new poem is written with the idea of Sappho. Although Shao starts finding the "new order" by focusing on rhythm and the structure influence of Western poetry, his focus gradually shifts to the influence of the ideas of Western poetry, which I will examine in the main body of my book.

In the scope of Western poetry, Shao had direct contact with Anglophone and Francophone poetry, and direct contact often entails a certain degree of influence. Shao's education at St John's, Cambridge and École des Beaux-Arts enabled him to read the first-hand material of Anglophone and Francophone poetry. Besides, as a publisher, he deserves commendation for introducing a great amount of Anglophone and Francophone authors to the Chinese readers. Some of these authors had never debuted in Chinese journals and Shao made full use of the three journals of which he served as the editor-in-chief (as mentioned in the biography section): *Sphinx Monthly*, *Sphinx Fortnightly* and *La Maison D'Or Monthly* to advocate the literary values that he sees in these authors. According to Wang Jingfang's 王京芳 study in *Shao Xunmei: Don Quixote in Publishing* (Shao Xunmei: chubanjie de Tangjikede 邵洵美: 出版界的堂吉柯德),[75] the translated works of the following Anglophone and Francophone authors frequently appear in his journals: Swinburne, Sitwell, Moore, Mallarmé, Baudelaire, Gautier, Verlaine, Huysmans, Rimbaud, the Pre-Raphaelites, Aubrey Beardsley,[76] Arthur Symons,[77] W. H. Davies,[78] Conrad

---

[75] Wang Jingfang 王京芳, *Shao xunmei: chubanjie de Tangjikede* 邵洵美: 出版界的堂吉柯德 [Shao Xunmei: Don Quixote in Publishing] (Guangzhou: Guangdong jiaoyu chubanshe, 2012).

[76] Aubrey Beardsley (1872-1898) was a British illustrator and writer. He is an important figure in the Aesthetic movement and his most notable work is his illustrations for Wilde's *Salome*.

[77] Arthur Symons (1865-1945) was a British poet and literary critic. His critically-acclaimed works include the poetry collection *Poems* (1902) and a monograph entitled *The Symbolist Movement in Literature* (1899).

[78] William Henry Davies (1871-1940) was a British writer. His most famous work is *The Autobiography of a Super-Tramp* (1908).

Aiken,[79] and Elinor Wylie.[80] From this list, one can get a glimpse at Shao's reading list and possible sources of influence.

Shao's publications serve as a platform to pass on the influence of the writers whom he applauds. His journals help introduce and circulate the works of many Western symbolist poets, which influenced a group of Chinese poets who are often labelled with Chinese symbolism, such as Feng Naichao 冯乃超,[81] Yu Gengyu 于赓虞[82] and Wang Duqing 王独清.[83] The Chinese symbolists never form any literary society, and they do not have a common journal as their loudspeaker. They are grouped by the affinity of their artistic propositions, which can be summarized by the following observation made by Mu Mutian 穆木天:[84]

> Poetry must have a huge potential to suggest. Though the world of poetry is in daily life, it is in the depth of daily life. Poetry must hint at the secrets of one's inner life. Poetry is suggestive, and it is most afraid of explanations. Explanation is something that belongs to the world of prose [...] It is poetry's basic instinct to reveal the unlimited world with limited rhythmic words.

> 诗是要有大的暗示能。诗的世界固在平常的生活中，但在平常生活的深处。诗是要暗示出人的内生命的深秘。诗要暗示的，诗最忌说明的。说

---

[79] Conrad Aiken (1889-1973) was an American writer. His notable works inlucde poetry collections *The Charnel Rose* (1918) and *Selected Poems* (1929).
[80] Elinor Wylie (1885-1928) was an American writer. Her critically-acclaimed works include the poetry collections *Nets to Catch the Wind* (1921) and *Black Armor* (1923).
[81] Feng Naichao (1901-1983) was a poet, art critic and social activist. He was born in Japan and educated in Kyoto Imperial University and Tokyo Imperial University. His most critically-acclaimed work is the poetry collection *Red Gauze Lantern* (Hong shadeng 红纱灯) (1928).
[82] Yu Gengyu (1902-1963) was a poet and translator who is often associated with the Crescent Moon Society. He was educated in the University of London.
[83] Wang Duqing (1898-1940) was a poet and literary critic. He was educated in Japan and France, though the names of the institutions are unknown. His critically-acclaimed works include the poetry collections *Before the Statue of Virgin Mary* (Shengmu xiangqian 圣母像前) (1927) and *Before Death* (Siqian 死前) (1927).
[84] Mu Mutian (1900-1971) was a poet and translator who is often considered one of the most important figures in Chinese symbolism. Educated in Tokyo University, he is most famous for his poetry collections *Journey to the Heart* (Lü xin 旅心) (1927), *The Song of the Refugee* (Liuwangzhe zhi ge 流亡者之歌) (1937) and *A New Journey* (Xinde lütu 新的旅途) (1942).

明是散文的世界里的东西 [...] 用有限的律动的字句启示出无限的世界是诗的本能。⁸⁵

Though Shao is usually not considered as a part of the cohort, his selection of Western authors in the journals where he serves as the editor-in-chief resonates with, and contributes to the popularity of Western symbolist poetry in the 20s. The introductions he makes and the translations he facilitates transmit the influence of the introduced and translated Western authors, who influenced him first, to a broader group of readers in Republican China. This is also the reason why Shao, when marginalized after 1949, was for a long time mentioned only as a publisher.

One might contend that the selection of these authors is not the sole decision of the editor-in-chief and that it could be subject to the contributions submitted and the preference of the other editors. Hence one might think that the authors introduced in the journals could not prove that Shao is familiar with and influenced by Anglophone literature. However, I would venture to say that Shao's knowledge of Anglophone literature is enormous. This is epitomized by an article published in 1929, where he introduces to the Chinese readers how the trend of Sappho recurs in Anglophone literature:

> Although Robert Herrick⁸⁶ quoted in a poem to his lover a fragment of Sappho that starts with "(a thing) much whiter than an egg", and though John Lyly⁸⁷ wrote *Sappho and Phao* to please Queen Elizabeth I, everything about Sappho was still vague [...] After 1711 there emerged more serious studies of Sappho. That year Joseph Addison⁸⁸ discussed

---

⁸⁵ Mu, "On Poetry" (Tanshi 谈诗), originally published in *Creation Monthly* (Chuangzao yuekan 创造月刊) Issue 1 (1926). Here quoted from *Zhongguo wenlunxuan, xiandaijuan (shang)* 中国文论选 现代卷 (上) [An Anthology of Chinese Literary Theories, the Modern Volume (1)], ed. Wang Yunxi 王运熙 (Nanjing: Jiangsu wenyi chubanshe, 1996), 456-457.
⁸⁶ Robert Herrick (1591-1674) was an English poet. His most notable work is the poetry collection *Hesperides* (1648), which features "To the Virgins, to Make Much of Time", one of the most famous carpe diem poems. In Republican China, the translated names of many foreign authors and literary associations were different from those that are commonly accepted now. In the excerpt Shao uses 海立克 (Hailike), and now he is usually known as 罗伯特·赫里克 (Luobote Helike).
⁸⁷ John Lyly (1553-1606) was an English dramatist and writer best known for the didactic romance *Euphues: The Anatomy of Wit* (1578). In the excerpt Shao refers to his name as 赖立 (Laili), and now he is usually known as 约翰·利利 (Yuehan Lili).
⁸⁸ Joseph Addison (1672-1719) was an English essayist and politician. He is remembered along with Richard Steele as the founder of *The Spectator* magazine. Shao in the excerpt

Sappho at length in his magazine. In 1748 Tobias Smollett[89] translated her second hymn [...] In 1814 Charles Abraham Elton[90] translated a lot of her fragments, and in 1815 there were the translations by Francis-Henry Egerton[91] [...] But the most acclaimed translations were those by J. A. Symonds[92] in 1883, and those published by Henry Thornton Wharton[93] in 1885.

虽然海立克写给他情人的诗中，引用过莎茀的那句"比蛋更白"的残诗，虽然赖立曾写过一本戏剧《莎茀与飞虹》以取悦衣里沙白皇后，但是对于莎茀的一切模糊得很 [...] 一七一一年以后，方才有人正式地研究莎茀。那年爱迪生在他编的报上，做了长文讨论。一七四八年，史马来脱又译了她的第二首颂歌 [...] 一八一四年衣而登译了她不少诗，一八一五年有衣辩登的译文 [...] 但是最受人称颂的是一八八三年西门子的译文，及一八八五年初版的华顿的一本莎茀诗译。[94]

This précis indicates that Shao is familiar with the literary history and jargon of Anglophone literature. The display of knowledge is again a proof that Shao was influenced by Anglophone literature. But as this book only investigates the influence of Anglophone writers on Shao when it comes to the condition of music in poetry, I will gently screen out the writers in Shao's reading list who do not talk about the condition of music in poetry. With the filter applied, I then rank the sifted names based on how frequently they are mentioned in Shao's works. In this fashion, three major sources are singled out: A. C. Swinburne, Edith Sitwell and George Moore. The following literature review will revolve around the influence of these authors on Shao.

---

refers to him as 爱迪生 (Aidisheng), and now he is usually known as 约瑟夫·艾迪生 (Yuesefu Aidisheng).

[89] Tobias Smollett (1721-1771) was a Scottish writer best known for his novels *The Adventures of Roderick Random* (1748) and *The Expedition of Humphry Clinker* (1771). Shao in the excerpt refers to him as 史马来脱 (Shimalaituo), and now he is usually known as 托比亚斯·斯摩莱特 (Tuobiyasi Simolaite).

[90] Charles Abraham Elton (1778–1853) was a British author.

[91] Francis Henry Egerton (1756-1829) was a British scholar.

[92] John Addington Symonds (1840-1893) was a British poet, literary critic and one of the early proponents of homosexuality.

[93] Henry Thornton Wharton (1846-1895) was a British scholar.

[94] Shao, "Sappho the Greek Sage Poet" (Xila nüshisheng Shafu 希腊女诗圣莎茀), originally published in *Zhenshanmei* (真善美) Special Issue on Female Writers (1929). Here quoted from *Collected Works of Shao Xunmei*, 179-181.

0.3 Shao and Anglophone influences

In the period of Republican China, there was no criticism that focuses on the influence of Anglophone literature on Shao, as the influence was still taking shape and it was hard to see the overall picture up-close. After 1949 there was a large blank in the poetry criticism on Shao. In February 1985, Shao's accusation of imperialist espionage was officially revoked by the government. An open discussion of his works became politically correct and hence viable. Li Guangde's 李广德 "On the Poetry and Poetics of Shao Xunmei" (Shilun Shao Xunmei de shi yu shilun 试论邵洵美的诗与诗论), written in April 1985, was the earliest critique on Shao after the vindication.[95] It is an attempt to render Shao's poetry visible again to critical attention and fill the blank that had been long ignored in 20th-century Chinese literary history. He writes:

> Shao Xunmei is an influential poet in the history of Chinese new poetry, a publisher and translator who made an extraordinary contribution to the development of Chinese new poetry and the introduction of foreign poetry to China. And yet people know little or nothing about such a poet, publisher and translator, about his creative path, poetic works, artistic propositions, about his achievements and contributions in publishing and translation.

> 邵洵美是中国新诗史上一个有影响的诗人,也是对中国新诗的发展和外国诗歌的介绍作出过显着贡献的出版家和翻译家。 然而对于这样一位诗人、出版家和翻译家,对于他的创作道路、诗歌作品、艺术主张、出版及译着的成就与贡献,人们不是一无所知就是所知甚少。[96]

In the article, Li gives a survey of Shao's education and points out the important influence of Swinburne on Shao's early poetry. Though the survey is comprehensive in width, it does not endeavor to excavate the depth of the influence and how the influence helps shape Shao's poetics.

In 1998 Xie Zhixi 解志熙 published "The Dissemination of British Aesthetic Literature in Modern China" (Yingguo weimeizhuyi wenxue zai xiandai

---

[95] Li Guangde 李广德, "Shilun Shao Xunmei de shi yu shilun" 试论邵洵美的诗与诗论 [On the Poetry and Poetics of Shao Xunmei], first published in *Huzhou shizhuan xuebao (shehuikexue ban)* 湖州师专学报 (社会科学版) [Journal of Huzhou Normal College (Social Science)] 1985, no.2: 1-9, and later in *Zhongguo xiandai wenxue yanjiu congshu* 中国现代文学研究丛书 [Modern Chinese Literature Studies] 1986, no.4: 58-73.
[96] Ibid., 58.

Zhongguo de chuanbo 英国唯美主义文学在现代中国的传播),[97] which touches upon the reception of Swinburne and Moore in China. He observes that Swinburne was widely read among the literati of Republican China and that "Shao Xunmei regards Swinburne as one of his 'two idols'."[98] ("邵洵美就把史文朋奉为自己的 '两个偶像' 之一。")[99] When it comes to Moore, Xie maintains that he was not sought after in China until Shao and his cohorts in Sphinx Club fervently introduced his works. He states that "Shao is an admirer of Moore and had correspondence with him." ("邵洵美是摩尔的崇拜者, 并与之有通信联系。")[100] Though Xie confirms Shao's role as an active propagator of these two authors in Republican China, he is more interested in the cultural diaspora of British aestheticism than its influence on the poetics of any particular Chinese poet. Similarly, in 2004 Sheng Xingjun 盛兴军 surveys Shao's agency in his reception of Anglophone and Francophone writers often labelled with aestheticism.[101] He writes: "Shao Xunmei is especially focused on the propagation of the British aestheticist Swinburne […] He also favors the hedonism of George Moore." ("邵洵美尤其注意对英国唯美主义作家史文朋的宣传 […] 他更偏爱乔治·摩尔的享乐主义。")[102] Swinburne and Moore are again clearly identified, though they are not treated at enough length and hence drowned in a long list of authors that might have had an influence on Shao. This 6-page article functions more as an index than an elaborated critique on Shao's reception of aestheticism.

In 2001 Jonathan Hutt published "*La Maison D'or* -The Sumptuous World of Shao Xunmei".[103] He claims that Shao's social pre-eminence "owed more to his personality and lifestyle than to his 'immoral' verse"[104] and that "Shao's status

---

[97] Xie Zhixi 解志熙, "Yingguo weimeizhuyi wenxue zai xiandai Zhongguo de chuanbo" 英国唯美主义文学在现代中国的传播 [The Dissemination of British Aesthetic Literature in Modern China], in *Waiguo wenxue pinglun* 外国文学评论 [Foreign Literature Review] 1998, no.1: 121-131.

[98] "Two Idols" (Liangge ouxiang 两个偶像) is an article Shao published in *La Maison D'Or Monthly* issue 5 (1929). The two idols refer to Swinburne and Sappho.

[99] Xie Zhixi, "The Dissemination of British Aesthetic Literature in Modern China", 122.

[100] Ibid., 128.

[101] Sheng Xingjun 盛兴军, "Tuifeizhe ji qixinyang—Shao Xunmei yu xifang weimeizhuyi" 颓废者及其信仰—邵洵美与西方"唯美主义" [A Decadent and His Faith—Shao Xunmei and Western Aestheticism], in *Shanghai daxue xuebao* 上海大学学报(社会科学版) [Journal of Shanghai University (Social Science)] 2004, vol. 11, no. 1: 39-45.

[102] Ibid., 43-44.

[103] Jonathan Hutt, "*La Maison D'or* -The Sumptuous World of Shao Xunmei", *East Asian History* 2001, no. 21: 111-142.

[104] Ibid., 112.

as a literary celebrity proved to be more enduring than his fame as a poet".[105] When it comes to Swinburne's influence on Shao, Hutt writes that "It was only to be expected that Swinburne would become a pivotal figure not simply in Shao's poetic career but also in the construction of his literary persona".[106] In general, Hutt is more obsessed with Shao's celebrity than celebrating the positive effect of poetry influence.

In 2006 Gao Wei 高蔚 interrogates the conceptions of "pure poetry" in Francophone and Anglophone symbolism as well as their diaspora in Republican China.[107] There are about 21 pages devoted to Shao's rendering of "pure poetry" and how it might have been influenced by Moore, which will be discussed in the third chapter of my book.

In 2014, Sun Jicheng 孙继成 and Hal Swindall engage with several poems of Shao and identify the similarities between Shao and Swinburne through close reading.[108] However, this 4-page article is restricted by its length and never goes beyond a general discussion of shared themes and symbols between the two poets.[109]

---

[105] Ibid., 132.
[106] Ibid., 115.
[107] Gao Wei 高蔚, "Chunshi jiqi zhongguohua yanjiu" 纯诗及其中国化研究 [A Study of 'Pure Poetry' and Its Reception in China], Diss. East China Normal University, 2006.
[108] Sun Jicheng 孙继成 and Hal Swindall, "Lun Yingguo shiren Shiwenpeng dui Shao Xunmei shige chuangzuo de yingxiang" 论英国诗人史文朋对邵洵美诗歌创作的影响) [Swinburne's Influence on the Poetry of Shao Xunmei], in *Shandong ligong daxue xuebao (shehuikexue ban)* 山东理工大学学报 (社会科学版) [Journal of Shandong University of Technology (Social Science)] 2014, vol. 30, no. 6: 50-54.
[109] In 2015 *The West in Asia and Asia in the West: Essays on Transnational Interactions* includes an article by Sun and Swindall entitled "A Chinese Swinburne: Shao Xunmei's Life and Art", which bears much resemblance to the previous article in Chinese. Sun Jicheng and Hal Swindall, "A Chinese Swinburne: Shao Xunmei's Life and Art", *The West in Asia and Asia in the West: Essays on Transnational Interactions*, ed. Elisabetta Marino, Tanfer Emin Tunc (Jefferson: McFarland, 2015), 133-146. It is likely that this article written in English is based on the one published in the Chinese journal.

In 2014 Chen Yue 陈越 surveys the dialogues among Shao, Qian Zhongshu 钱钟书 [110] and Xing Guangzu 邢光祖 [111] in the 30s and 40s regarding the commensurability of the conceptions of "texture" and *jili* 肌理 as proposed by Edith Sitwell and Weng Fanggang 翁方纲 [112] respectively. [113] This will be discussed in the second chapter, which concerns Sitwell's influence on Shao.

In 2015 Paul Bevan illustrates how a group of Shanghai-based cartoonists were influenced by some of their foreign peers in the 30s, and delineates a profile of Shao, who is indispensable for getting these artists together. [114] Throughout the book, Shao's contact with Anglophone literature is frequently mentioned, and the second chapter named "Shao Xunmei and His Circle" gives a sketch of how Shao came to know the name of Swinburne. However, given the fact that the book deals so exclusively with the realm of interwar cartoons, the profile of Shao never gets any deeper than personal anecdotes. Therefore it is of limited use to my research.

In 2016 Yue Daiyun 乐黛云 published *China and the West at the Crossroads: Essays on Comparative Literature and Culture*, which features a

---

[110] Qian Zhongshu (1910-1998) was one of the most famous 20th century Chinese literary critics and a frequently-studied prose writer. Educated in Tsinghua and Oxford University, he was familiar with Chinese classical literature, and obtained language proficiency in Latin, French, Spanish, Italian as well as English and German. His critical works are esoteric, with frequent allusions to a profusion of Chinese and Western texts. Some examples are *On the Edge of Life* (Xiezai rensheng bianshang 写在人生边上), a collection of critical essays published in 1941, and *On Arts* (Tan yi lu 谈艺录), a critical anthology written in classical Chinese and published in 1948. His prose works, as epitomized by the well-acclaimed novel *Fortress Besieged* (Weicheng 围城) (1947), often demonstrate a wrestling between the conventional Chinese concerns about ethics and an awareness of the ontological crisis that becomes increasingly prominent in the 20th century.

[111] Xing Guangzu (1914-1993) was a writer and politician. He was educated in Guanghua University and Far Eastern University in Manila. His most notable work is the poetry collection *Guangzu's Poems* (Guangzu de shi 光祖的诗) (1937).

[112] Weng Fanggang (1733-1818) was an author, epigraphist and literary critic in Qing Dynasty. He was famous for his conception of Jili 肌理 in poetry criticism and also for his achievements in textology, epigraphy and calligraphy.

[113] Chen Yue 陈越, "Zhongguo xiandai shixue zhong de jilishuo" 中国现代诗学中的"肌理说" [On the Theory of Texture in Modern Chinese Poetics], in *Zhongguo xiandai wenxue yanjiu congkan* 中国现代文学研究丛刊 [Modern Chinese Literature Studies] 2014, no.3: 107-121.

[114] Paul Bevan, *A Modern Miscellany: Shanghai Cartoon Artists, Shao Xunmei's Circle and the Travels of Jack Chen, 1926-1938* (Leiden: Brill, 2015).

chapter entitled "The Last Decadent in China: Shanghai's Shao Xunmei".[115] Swinburne and Moore are again identified as two major sources of Shao's inspirations. But as this chapter only functions as a small puzzle piece for a much bigger picture that this book intends to draw, the connections between Shao and the two authors are not thoroughly scrutinized.

0.4 Shao and music

In a review of Moore's *Pure Poetry: An Anthology*, Shao points out that "what Moore terms as pure poetry is something that must rid itself of concepts and meanings; but by no means would he conclude that 'poetry is music'. He only claims that there is a certain amount of homogeneity between poetry and music" ("Moore 所谓的纯粹的诗是须离开观念与意思的; 但他决不便说 '诗是音乐'。他只是说诗与音乐有相同的地方").[116] This "certain amount" is, however, uncertain and highly ambiguous. The attempt to clarify such ambiguity has been evident in the research of musicopoetics, an interdisciplinary study and a study of interdisciplinarity in reaction to the Cartesian framing of disciplines. The following pages serve as a historical survey of this interdisciplinary study.

In the 1980s, Steven Paul Scher observed that the research of musicopoetics had become "a popular field of interdisciplinary inquiry among both musicologists and literary critics" and it "fares well in the critical climate of post-modernism, deconstruction, and semiotics" while conceding that "few if any recent musico-literary studies have broken new critical ground",[117] which resonates with Laurence Kramer's lament that "twentieth-century advances in literary interpretation and musical analysis have done little to foster an interdisciplinary method".[118]

To deal with the void of theoretical apparatus, Kramer attempts to establish in *Music and Poetry: The Nineteenth Century and After* "a discipline that could situate the two arts in a coherent and significant context"[119] and "bring poetry and music into a single discourse"[120] through "new ways of reading and

---

[115] Yue Daiyun 乐黛云, *China and the West at the Crossroads: Essays on Comparative Literature and Culture,* trans. Geng Song and Darrell Dorrington (Beijing: Springer, 2016).
[116] Shao, "Pure Poetry" (Chuncui de shi 纯粹的诗), *Collected Works of Shao Xunmei*, 184.
[117] Steven Paul Scher, Rev. of *Music and Poetry: The Nineteenth Century and After, 19th-Century Music* 10.3 (1987): 290.
[118] Lawrence Kramer, *Music and Poetry: The Nineteenth Century and After* (London: University of California Press, 1984), 4.
[119] Ibid., vii.
[120] Ibid., 8.

hearing",[121] so as to interrogate "when and how a poem and a composition can be discussed in tandem [...] not just in a general way, but in enough detail to support an extended consideration of both".[122] The book is applauded by Scher as "imaginative in conception, innovative in critical method, seminal in its analytical results, and coherently argued",[123] though Rudolf Arnheim regards it as a "conceptual rarefaction at which the practitioners of neither music nor poetry commonly dwell".[124]

This inter-ness where "the practitioners of neither music nor poetry commonly dwell"[125] is indeed Kramer's major concern, which he terms as interart convergence. His emphasis, as Scher observes, is "how and under what circumstances convergences of music and poetry manifest themselves".[126] Kramer deems such convergence as a gestural process;[127] he designates the term "gestural" as an "idea that music and poetry, more than any of the other arts, define their formal shape as a function of rhythmically integrated time".[128]

Kramer's central argument is that "a poem and a composition may converge on a structural rhythm: that a shared pattern of unfolding can act as an interpretive framework for the explicit dimension of both works",[129] which, as Scher observes, is a synthesis of Edward T. Cone's claim that musical form is rhythmic and Barbara Herrnstein Smith's proposal that poetic structure is "consisting of the principles by which [a poem] is generated or according to which one element follows another".[130]

Reiterating that structural rhythm is central to musicopoetic convergence, Kramer claims that "once a feeling for structural rhythm plays a part in reading and listening, convergences begin to suggest themselves".[131] This synoptic view, as Scher maintains, is a possible approach to "talk meaningfully about

---

[121] Ibid., vii.
[122] Ibid., 4.
[123] Scher, Rev. of *Music and Poetry: The Nineteenth Century and After*, 290.
[124] Rudolf Arnheim, Rev. of *Music and Poetry: The Nineteenth Century and After*, *The Musical Quarterly* 71.3 (1985): 379.
[125] Rudolf Arnheim, Rev. of *Music and Poetry: The Nineteenth Century and After*, *The Musical Quarterly* 71.3 (1985): 379.
[126] Scher, Rev. of *Music and Poetry: The Nineteenth Century and After*, 290.
[127] Kramer, *Music and Poetry: The Nineteenth Century and After*, vii.
[128] Ibid., 30.
[129] Ibid., 10.
[130] Scher, Rev. of *Music and Poetry: The Nineteenth Century and After*, 290.
[131] Kramer, *Music and Poetry: The Nineteenth Century and After*, 24.

specific works of music and poetry in tandem, without succumbing to sheer impressionism".¹³²

The conception of structural rhythm resembles Sitwell's proposal of poetic texture, which Shao summarizes as: "The intonation of words and the configuration of lines and stanzas are closely connected to the expression and revelation of a poem's meaning" ("字眼的音调形式, 句段的长短分合, 与诗的内容意义的表现及点化上, 有密切之关系").¹³³ However, is "musicality" in poetry merely a matter of pattern that resembles musical composition, or it could be something else?

In the new millennium, Eric Prieto wrote in *Listening In: Music, Mind, and the Modernist Narrative* that music and poetry in the 19th century are "no longer considered to be linked through voice and performance but through the internalized, metaphorical voice that Mallarmé calls L'Idée. Music, in other words, has become available as a metaphor that embodies a type of thought, not a type of performance".¹³⁴ The metaphorical use of music, as Joseph Acquisto observes, is an "eternal textual and conceptual restlessness, or even homelessness, that is of most use in characterizing symbolism, a notoriously difficult movement to define precisely".¹³⁵ Prieto states that "what literature can borrow from music is not actual tones or rhythm or a model of poetic diction but a model of semantic autonomy, a mode of signification that does not limit thought to the denotata of words", which is, to "signify without naming".¹³⁶ This begins with the metaphoricalization of the concept "music", which "refers to a mode of thought that owes little to actual musical composition apart from the abstract principles of pattern and proportion, which are taken to be in competition with the grammatical and semantic rules that govern normal linguistic statements".¹³⁷ In a genealogical manner, he traces the marriage of music and poetry back to the Greeks "who grouped music and poetry together, along with dance, under the heading mousike".¹³⁸ He asserts that "music, along with such musico-poetic devices as rhythm, meter, and motivic repetition, played an important role in helping performers

---

132 Scher, Rev. of *Music and Poetry: The Nineteenth Century and After*, 292.
133 Shao, "New Poetry and 'Texture'" (Xinshi yu jili 新诗与"肌理"), *Collected Works of Shao Xunmei*, 135.
134 Eric Prieto, *Listening In: Music, Mind, and the Modernist Narrative* (Lincoln: University of Nebraska Press, 2002), 8.
135 Joseph Acquisto, *French Symbolist Poetry and the Idea of Music* (Burlington: Ashgate, 2006), 2.
136 Prieto, *Listening In: Music, Mind, and the Modernist Narrative*, 8.
137 Ibid., 11.
138 Ibid., 1.

remember and pass on the traditional tales that constitute the primary repositories of historical and cultural memory in oral communities".[139]

The appearance of writing and print technology, and the subsequent specialization of music and poetry practitioners have caused that "the traditional relationship between the two arts, in song, had begun to erode".[140] The "song" here, as Kramer observes, is "a form of synthesis [...] the art that reconciles music and poetry, intonation and speech, as means of expression".[141] This erosion has triggered some concerns that "poetry, relegated to the page, will lose its voice, while music, cast adrift from its traditional verbal and contextual meanings, will stop making sense".[142] In reaction to these concerns, Wagner's Gesamtkunstwerk is an attempt to revive the Greek mousike and reconglomerate music and poetry. However, the twentieth century has gone through further distancing of music and poetry, as Kramer observes, "the gradual formalization of technique in each discipline, with its concomitant specialization, has drawn attention away from issues surrounding words and music that the nineteenth century found compelling".[143]

Shao is deeply influenced by the nineteenth-century Francophone and Anglophone poetry, and therefore Prieto's *Listening In: Music, Mind, and the Modernist Narrative* is of particular use to my research. I would venture to say that structure is not the word Shao has in mind when he talks about music in poetry. The works of Shao give no hints about his ability to compose, play musical instruments or analyze music in a musicological way. However, there are accounts that show his fondness for listening to music, such as his reverie at a Schubert concert:

> After the andante con moto of the C major symphony, the scherzo allegro vivace begins. It's like after the inexperienced girl leaves, the bawdiest woman starts telling her five or six friends about the ecstasy, horror and shame on her wedding night. She's not afraid someone might be listening through the wall; she speaks so loud that everyone laughs, holding their stomachs.
>
> Twenty, thirty violin bows shoot into a pond like heavy thunder rain or sharp arrows, pouring and plucking rapidly. The conductor stands

---

[139] Ibid., 2.
[140] Ibid., 1.
[141] Kramer, *Music and Poetry: The Nineteenth Century and After*, 125.
[142] Ibid., 2.
[143] Ibid., 14.

among the violinists like a tree amid a thunderstorm, swaying to the east one moment, pressed to the west the next and then standing straight again [...] I'm not a musician, nor someone who knows music; but I don't think I could do without it. When I hear waving, slowly flowing, shaking, tumbling, floating…I feel a sense that I can't express in words. At that moment, music becomes the God of my senses and my soul.

C调长音阶交响曲的 Andante con moto 以后，Scherzo allegro vivace 便开场了。正像是当一个未经人事的小姑娘离开后，那惯常最诙谐的少妇便开始对着五六个知己讲她从前新婚床上的狂欢、恐怖与羞惭，但她却不怕有人在隔墙偷听，她讲得很高，引得什么人都笑了，什么人都捧着肚子。

二三十支 Violin 的弦杆便像骤急的雷雨利箭般射入水潭的里面，高速度的倾入与弹起；那 Conductor 站在 Violinists 的中间，便像一棵雷雨中的小树，忽而压到了东，忽而压到了西，忽而又竖了起来 [...] 我不是个乐师，更不是个懂得音乐的；我也并不觉得我不能缺少了他：但当我听得了波动、缓流、激荡、狂翻、轻飘…时，我也自会感到一种说不出的兴味来。那时的音乐竟能变成我感官与心灵的一刹那的上帝。[144]

The identification of *andante con moto* and *scherzo allegro vivace* suggests that Shao is not unfamiliar with musical jargon. However, it is not known to what extent Shao understands the structure of musical compositions. He is commenting on an actual musical performance but these comments are not done through the same medium of musical performance—he is certainly not singing out his comments. As he tries to reproduce the significance that he perceives at the concert, he can only do it with words. And the description of the loud and funny woman, the thunderstorm and the waving, flowing, floating, is a metaphorical attempt to reproduce the perceived musical significance. As the attempt is metaphorical, it is in the realm of idea. The works to be studied in the main body of this book are not descriptions of any musical performance, or any verses that try to imitate the structure of musical compositions. What will be studied are poems that aspire to the condition of music, which is fundamentally an idea. This book endeavors to analyze this condition by engaging with the poems up-close, scrutinizing what Shao's idea of the condition of music in poetry denotes, and examining whether these poems fulfill their aspiration.

---

[144] Shao, "A Night of Schubert" (Schubert zhi yiye Schubert 之一夜), *Buneng shuohuang de zhiye* 不能说谎的职业 [A Job that Can't Lie] (Shanghai: Shanghai shudian chubanshe, 2012), 8-9.

As gender features a prominent place in Shao's idea of the condition of music in poetry, Ellen Koskoff's *A Feminist Ethnomusicology: Writings on Music and Gender* provides some helpful insights. She writes:

> Works began to appear in the 1970s that questioned the lack of women's representation in the literature as performers, creators, and experiencers of music cross-culturally […] A new form of music scholarship emerged that was heavily influenced by anthropology and social and cultural history, one that sought to understand music not simply as a product of human behavior, but also as an interpretive site for enacting and performing gender relations. A proliferation of studies on Western concert music, especially opera, as well as on Western or Western-influenced popular music traditions emerged at this time, as scholars began to expose powerful ideologies and systems of power that controlled gendered musical behavior and its discourses worldwide.[145]

One of the works that expose such "powerful ideologies and systems of power that controlled gendered musical behavior and its discourses" is Regula Hohl Trillini's survey of the performance on keyboard instruments and its gender ramifications from the Tudor period to the Great War in *The Gaze of the Listener: English Representations of Domestic Music-Making*. She states in the book:

> Gender […] is deeply inscribed into the musical mind-body dichotomy. The enduring, abstract arts of musical theory and composition were for a long time encoded as privileged and 'masculine', while performance with its inevitable involvement of the body was closely aligned with social inferiority, the alien exotic and, most of all, women.[146]

This observation upholds Lucy Green's statement in *Music, Gender, Education* that performing music at the time renders the players' "discursive position as feminine".[147] This, however, might only be true at certain social and temporal coordinates. When it comes to spaces and times outside the combined filters of "Britain" and "from Tudor period to the Great War", Koskoff states that "Descriptions of women performing musical instruments are relatively rare in the literature".[148] She writes:

---

[145] Ellen Koskoff, *A Feminist Ethnomusicology: Writings on Music and Gender* (Urbana: University of Illinois Press, 2014), 26-27.
[146] Regula Hohl Trillini, *The Gaze of the Listener: English Representations of Domestic Music-Making*, Word and Music Studies, Volume 10 (New York: Rodopi, 2008), 1.
[147] Lucy Green, *Music, Gender, Education* (Cambridge: Cambridge, 1997), 26.
[148] Koskoff, *A Feminist Ethnomusicology: Writings on Music and Gender*, 124.

In many societies, musical roles are divided along gender lines: women sing and men play. Of course, men also sing, and women sometimes play; yet, unlike men, women who play often do so in contexts of sexual and social marginality.[149]

[…]

Musical instruments are generally linked to gender ideologies, however culturally constructed and maintained. Such ideologies underlie and prescribe who can and cannot play and under what circumstances performances will occur. Thus, on the one hand, it appears that the instruments and sounds associated with men and with masculinity (however defined) are frequently linked to economic, ritual, and sexual power. Such instruments are often used by men to limit, control, or coerce women (or to heighten their own sexuality, as in rock performances).[150]

Hohl Trillini writes: "Women musicians have been represented as visual and acoustic objects of temptation and consumption, but also as the ennobling Saint Cecilia who draws the listener towards Heaven." [151] Both of these representations are present in Shao's poetry: "the ennobling Saint Cecilia who draws the listener towards Heaven" is similar to the way Shao renders Sappho in his poems, which I will discuss in the first chapter.

"Visual and acoustic objects of temptation and consumption" are on the other hand how Shao treats the flower-women in his poetry with his unique practice of "the horticulture of sisters", which will be examined in the second chapter. Hohl Trillini writes: "The gaze of the listener, of the narrator and of the implied reader is always the gaze of a male resting on the female object of his desire. Even the rare texts which represent women playing for themselves remind us that music is an opportunity for display because they usually imply an absent male lover."[152] This observation is particularly useful when it comes to the examination of Shao's visual exploitation of women and his s(t)imulation of sex in the flower-women poems. This kind of visual exploitation is considered by Hohl Trillini as something similar to cinematic communication. She cites from Mieke Bal that it tends to "reduce looking to power only, to an

---

[149] Ibid., 122.
[150] Ibid., 129.
[151] Hohl Trillini, *The Gaze of the Listener: English Representations of Domestic Music-Making*, 2.
[152] Ibid., 9.

absolute subject-object relation, wherein the viewer/receiver has total power and the object of the look does not even participate in the communication. This model is in fact based on noncommunication. (Bal, 383)" [153] Shao's s(t)imulation of sex through the visual display of the flower-women is such a non-communicating erotica. Hohl Trillini writes:

> One very effective way of ensuring noncommunication from women players is the metaphorical convention of equalling them with music, as exemplified in the *incipit* of Shakespeare's Sonnet 128 "Thou, My Music". This topos exalts and celebrates women but also deprives them of their voice and of communicative agency.[154]

The deprivation of women's voice and their communicative agency is indeed what happens to Shao's flower-women poems written under a synthesized influence of Sitwell. However, Hohl Trillini identifies the problem, but does not seem to provide any possible strategies of change and resistance. In the third chapter of my book, which dwells on Shao's reception of Moore's idea of pure poetry, there will be an examination of Shao's replacement of the dialectic of the body with the dialogic of voices, as well as a change of the way women are presented in his poetry, which might be an option for combating the tyranny of the male gaze in the realm of poetry.

It should be noted that here in the excerpt Hohl Trillini uses Shakespeare's Sonnet 128, a piece of poetry, to illustrate her point. She writes: "Poetry generally favours a metaphorical discourse of music and eschews its realities, just as the Petrarchan tradition elevates woman to an unreal and unreachable degree of perfection."[155] "A metaphorical discourse of music" is indeed what this book is about, as Shao's idea of the condition of music in poetry can be seen as a metaphor that unites music and poetry. In this regard, Hohl Trillini's analysis of Shakespeare's Sonnet 128 is of much pertinence to my research. She frequently uses this poem to talk about the womanization of instruments and the instrumentalization of women, which is particularly relevant to Shao's instrumentalization of women examined in the second chapter of my book. In the first chapter of her book "Sex and the Virginals: Gender and Keyboards around 1600", her observations on the playfulness of virginals' jacks and keys and "the mixed metaphors that tangle between player's body and instrument

---

[153] Hohl Trillini, *The Gaze of the Listener*, 10; Mieke Bal, "His Master's Eye", *Modernity and the Hegemony of Vision*, ed. David Michael Levin (Berkeley: University of California Press, 1993).
[154] Hohl Trillini, *The Gaze of the Listener*, 10.
[155] Ibid., 22.

Introduction xlv

[…] in [Shakespeare's] Sonnet 128"[156] are inspiring. The latter also provides an example of how to analyze a woman's music-making and its gender ramifications through close reading, which is also the methodology I chose.

In the first chapter of my book, which will discuss Swinburne and Shao's shared practice of cleaving Sappho to the nightingale, Sappho/the nightingale-woman plays the lyre. She is the player, and her instrument is the lyre. In Shao's early poems influenced by Swinburne, it seems that one can still distinguish the woman player from the instrument. As Shao's poetics gradually assimilate the influence of Sitwell, which is the focus of my second chapter, the woman becomes the instrument and Shao considers the male poet as the player. These two parts can all draw inspirations from Hohl Trillini's monograph. In the third chapter of my book, which discusses Shao's replacement of the dialectic of the body with the dialogic of voices, both the player and the instrument disappear. What remains are voices that are void of polemical relations. This is a part of which her book might be less helpful.

Due to the overall scarcity of secondary material on Shao, there is so far no criticism that deals exclusively with Shao's idea of the condition of music in poetry. In 2003 Ho Yeon Sung published *A Comparative Study of Shao Xunmei's Poetry*.[157] This is a monograph based on her master's dissertation at the Ohio State University and it features a discussion of lyricism in Shao's *Fire and Flesh*. However, the lyricism discussed here is reduced to a kind of sensibility and ability to express feelings. Its correlation with music is only given a few lines about the etymology of the word lyre in Greek. That being said, in all the secondary material on Shao, the adoption of the lens of lyricism already makes this book by far the closest to a discussion of Shao's idea of the condition of music in poetry.

The shortage of secondary material on Shao and music has certainly been a hindrance to my research. This is a path that has not been trodden. But on the other hand, this path promises a gap in the field that is in need of much original research. This book brings feminist skepticism to the scholarship of Shao, a male poet born, raised and having lived in colonial Shanghai. This feminist skepticism questions the conceptions of gender saturated in Shao's idea of the condition of music in poetry.

---

[156] Ibid., 24.
[157] Ho Yeon Sung, *A Comparative Study of Shao Xunmei's Poetry* (Columbus: Ohio State University Press, 2003).

0.5 A feminist approach

When talking about the new critical trends of "the large literature that exists on Music", Edward Said writes in *Musical Elaborations*:

> We do know more about the way cultures operate thanks to Raymond Williams, Roland Barthes, Michel Foucault, and Stuart Hall; we know about how to examine a text in ways that Jacques Derrida, Hayden White, Frederic Jameson, and Stanley Fish have significantly expanded and altered; and thanks to feminists like Elaine Showalter, Germaine Greer, Helene Cixous, Sandra Gilbert, Susan Gubar, and Gayatri Spivak it is impossible to avoid or ignore the gender issues in the production and interpretation of art.[158]

This comment, with its juxtaposition of laudations, seems harmless and "politically correct" at first glance. However, Susan Bordo points out that such a statement is characteristic of a construction that is "not merely an annoying bit of residual sexism, but a powerful conceptual map which keeps feminist scholarship, no matter how broad its concerns, located in the region of what Simone de Beauvoir called 'the Other'".[159] She writes:

> So: Because of Barthes, Derrida et al., we "know more" about culture and texts; "Thanks to feminists," we are unable to "avoid" or "ignore" gender [...] What I do want to insist on [...] is the importance of Said's juxtaposition of "gender" - what all feminists are concerned with, in his description - and the general interrogation of "culture" and "text" attributed to the men. The juxtaposition situates feminists as engaging in a specialized critique, one which cannot be ignored, perhaps, but one whose implications are contained, self-limiting, and of insufficient general consequence to amount to a new knowledge of "the way culture operates." [...] Said's juxtaposition of those writers who teach us "about the way culture operates" and those who make it "impossible to avoid or ignore gender issues" applauds the feminist - as Other.[160]

Bordo writes: "We remain the Other in the self-conception of our discipline, in intellectual history generally, and even in narratives about the very changes that we brought about."[161] She contends that the cultural ideology and

---

[158] Edward Said, *Musical Elaborations* (London: Chatto & Windus, 1991), 11.
[159] Susan Bordo, "The Feminist as Other", *Metaphilosophy* 1996, vol. 27, no. 1-2: 12.
[160] Ibid., 11-12.
[161] Ibid., 23.

disciplinary practice renders the male body as "'The Body' proper", disappearing completely, "its concrete specificity submerged in its collapse into the universal", "while the female body remains marked by its difference".[162] She states: "Thus, while men are the cultural theorists of the body, only women have bodies. Meanwhile, of course, the absent male body continues to operate illicitly as the (scientific, philosophical, medical) norm for all."[163] She argues that this normalizing, universal male body does not change much from the ideas of Descartes to the postmodern critiques written by male theorists.[164]

Bordo's works, as epitomized by *Unbearable Weight: Feminism, Western Culture, and the Body*[165] and *The Flight to Objectivity: Essays on Cartesianism and Culture*[166], have influenced my research. The influence of her works does not simply take the form of my adoption and application of certain terms and concepts that she proposes onto my examination process of the primary material that I chose and the formation of my argument as well as the conclusion. The major influence might be that I derive a synthesized idea from my reception of her works that the body is a metaphor and that the metaphoricity of the body enables various possibilities of talking about technology, epistemology, and in the case of my book, how the condition of music in poetry can be produced.

The methodology that I chose for this book, or I should say method that does not intend to establish itself as an authoritative "-ology", is close reading with "feminist skepticism" that pays attention to what Bordo calls the "hermeneutics of suspicion".[167] She writes: "Gender bias may be revealed in one's perspective on the nature of reality, in one's style of thinking, in one's approach to problems—quite apart from any explicit gender content or attitudes toward the sexes."[168] Shao's gender bias in his reception of the Anglophone influences and his conception of the condition of music in poetry will be the primary focus of this feminist skepticism, and it will be addressed mainly in the second and third chapter of my book. "Explicit gender content or

---

[162] Ibid., 15.
[163] Ibid.
[164] Ibid., 24-25.
[165] Susan Bordo, *Unbearable Weight: Feminism, Western Culture, and the Body* (Berkeley: University of California Press, 1993).
[166] Susan Bordo, *The Flight to Objectivity: Essays on Cartesianism and Culture* (New York: SUNY Press, 1987).
[167] Susan Bordo, "Feminist Skepticism and the 'Maleness' of Philosophy", *The Journal of Philosophy* 1988, vol. 85, no. 11: 619.
[168] Ibid.

attitudes toward the sexes" in Shao's works, including but not limiting to what Bordo calls "objectionable images of women, misogynist theory, the lack of representation of women's concerns and voices"[169] will also be scrutinized as a secondary task.

This book consists of three chapters. Each chapter will deal with one Anglophone writer and his/her influence on Shao's idea of the condition of music in poetry. Through close reading I will identify the sources of influence, locate any evidence for such influence and examine how the influence helps shape Shao's idea of the condition of music in poetry. The evidence for influence that I derive from the process of close reading will also be supported by some external evidence when it is appropriate.

Chapter 1 will focus on Swinburne's conception of harmony and its influence on Shao. Swinburne's influence on Shao took place in the 20s. The chapter will start from Shao's encounter with Sappho, an indispensable link between Shao and Swinburne. Then the chapter will look at how Shao came to know the works of Swinburne through Sappho and will examine how Shao's zest for Swinburne led him to the career of a poet. What follows is a survey of Swinburne's conception of harmony, inner music and outer music. The next section will be an investigation of the nightingale as a symbol of harmony used in both Shao and Swinburne's works. The last part of the chapter will scrutinize a shared practice between Shao and Swinburne, the merging of Sappho with the symbol of the nightingale.

Chapter 2 will focus on Sitwell's idea of poetry as "the sister of horticulture" and its influence on Shao. As Swinburne's influence on Shao gradually waned in the early 30s, Sitwell's influence began to take shape. The chapter will start with a survey of Sitwell's conception of "the sister of horticulture" and "texture". Then the chapter will look at a comparison between Shao's understanding of "texture" and *jili* 肌理, a Chinese term borrowed from the theory of an 18th-century literary critic Weng Fanggang (1733-1818). What comes after the comparison will be an examination of the use of the symbol of the flower in the poetry of Shao and Sitwell. I will look at Shao's idiosyncratic departure from Sitwell's notion of "the sister of horticulture", which I will venture to call "the horticulture of sisters", a unique practice of merging flower symbol with woman's body. What follows is an investigation of Shao's conception that the sexual consummation with the flower-woman is concurrently a condition of music in poetry. The last part of the chapter will scrutinize Shao's instrumentalisation of a woman's body and its negation of woman's agency.

---

[169] Ibid.

Chapter 3 will focus on Moore's idea of pure poetry and its influence on Shao. Moore and Shao started exchanging letters in the 20s, but his influence on Shao was not prominent until the mid-30s, when it was assimilated and synthesized by Shao with that of Swinburne and Sitwell. The chapter will start with an examination of Shao's correspondence with Moore and move into an investigation of Moore's conception of pure poetry, where the categories of poetry and music dissolve. I will look at Moore's proposal of the removal of the conception of the body as a means to achieve pure poetry, and examine how Shao puts the proposal into practice by replacing the dialectic of the body with the dialogic of voices. This replacement witnesses a tremendous change in Shao's attitude towards women. I will examine the woman's emancipation from being the instrumentalized other of "I" and its correlations to the freeing of music's fixation as something other than poetry. The last part will study how Shao receives Moore's conception of pure poetry as the ideal, primordial unity of arts, where poetry and music will always be in a dialogic process with no definite closure.

0.6 Translation policy

As this book is a comparative project whose primary material is written in Chinese, a language different from the language of the book, which is English, translation is adopted to ensure that this book can reach Anglophone readers who might not be familiar with the language of Chinese.

An aspect that complicates this practice is that the main subject of my book is poetry, and therefore most of the translations in this book are poetry translations. Lawrence Venuti points out that "poetry may well be the least translated literary genre [...] the marginality is, in fact, the first reason to move poetry closer to the center of translation studies".[170] He states that translation studies itself is often neglected for "its offense against the prevailing concept of authorship".[171] He writes:

> Translation provokes the fear of inauthenticity, distortion, contamination [...] translation is also an offense against a still prevailing concept of scholarship that rests on the assumption of original authorship [...] translation provokes the fear of error, amateurism, opportunism [...] Under the burden of these fears, translation has long been neglected in the study of literature, even in our current situation, where the influx of

---

[170] Lawrence Venuti, *Translation Changes Everything: Theory and Practice* (London: Routledge, 2013), 173.
[171] Venuti, *The Scandals of Translation: Towards an Ethics of Difference* (New York: Routledge, 1998), 31.

poststructuralist thinking has decisively questioned author-oriented literary theory and criticism.¹⁷²

Venuti's observations are reminiscent of an interesting translation practice of Shao. W. H. Auden and Christopher Isherwood visited China during the Sino-Japanese War in 1938. In June, Helen Foster Snow introduced them to Shao, who was then asked whether there was a good poem about the ongoing war. Shao claimed that there was a nice folk poem and he provided Auden and Isherwood with "Song of the Chinese Guerrilla Units" as the English translation, which was later featured in Auden and Isherwood's *Journey to a War*. Yet in *My Father Shao Xunmei*, Shao Xiaohong states that there is no such thing as the original of "Song of the Chinese Guerrilla Units" since Shao wrote the poem directly in English before he translated it back into Chinese and published it in *Pool of Freedom* (September 1938) under the name "Anonymous". This sheds some light on Shao's unorthodox views towards originality and translation.

Though Shao and his creative practices at times do not uphold the concept of authorship, this book is not a product of creative writing and it follows academic conventions. As translation is adopted in my book, the selection criteria of translations and their translators need to be addressed. Shao's works are scarcely translated into English. When I started drafting my book in 2015, there was no translated anthology of Shao's poems in English. In 2016 Sun and Swindall published *The Verse of Shao Xunmei*, the first English translation of Shao's poetry.¹⁷³ Strangely, this anthology forgoes *Flower-like Evil* and only includes *Heaven and May* and *Twenty-five Poems*. Besides, there are occasional errors in the translations. One example would be the line 17 of "Anch'io sono pittore!", where *Baotelei* 包特蕾 should be translated as Baudelaire instead of Gordon Bottomley¹⁷⁴ (there is even a typo here as it is printed as "Gorden" Bottomley).¹⁷⁵ Last but not least, the translations prioritize semantic clarity over poetic equivalence, and hence become bland and unpoetic.

Considering its strange editorial decision of omitting *Flower-like Evil*, the minor errors in the translations and its failure in doing justice to Shao's poetic caliber, I eventually decided to translate the poems myself. In addition to the poems, all the Chinese texts quoted in this book pertaining to Shao's life and works are translated by me unless otherwise specified. All the English translations I make in the book will be immediately followed by the original

---

¹⁷² Ibid.
¹⁷³ Sun Jicheng and Hal Swindall, *The Verse of Shao Xunmei* (Paramus: Homa & Sekey Books, 2016).
¹⁷⁴ Gordon Bottomley (1874-1948) was a British poet.
¹⁷⁵ Ibid., 110.

Introduction

quotes in Chinese, which are open for scrutinization from readers who are familiar with both languages.

In my translations, I keep the same punctuations used in the Chinese texts, though the usage of punctuation might not always be deemed correct in English grammar. One example is the use of commas. Shao in his poems tends to use a series of commas to link multiple clauses with no conjunctions used. This is acceptable in Chinese grammar, but not in English grammar. However, though it is not correct according to English grammar, keeping the commas does not do harm to the signification of the lines. Therefore I keep the commas in my translations.

Chapter 1

Shao, Swinburne and the idea of harmony

1.1 The gathering of Shao, Sappho and Swinburne

1.1.1 Shao's encounter with Sappho

In the winter of 1924, the eighteen-year-old Shao went to Cambridge for higher education. As the ship called at Naples, he took some time to savour the cultural scenes of the city and accidentally came across the name of Sappho, who later became his lifetime muse and an indispensable link to Swinburne. In an article published five years later, Shao recalls this unchoreographed yet almost destined encounter:

> It was my second day in Naples. After lunch I walked to the National Archeological Museum alone […] As I marveled at the collections my eyes were suddenly drawn, by a force unknown, to a fragmented fresco. This fresco is but two feet in length and about one foot in width, but the painted beauty seemed to be talking to me with a gaze as if at her lovers: come to me, my Xunmei! —Ah, I was drunk! I was numb! I was seduced! How could I go to her? And where would I go to get to her? To her heart, yes her heart is cold. If I went to her soul, my own soul would be quite lost […] The guard suddenly seemed kinder, smiled and said in Italian English: "This is Sappho, a poetess of Greece."
>
> "Ah she is also a poet. Scary! Lovely!" It is a silent sentence jerked out of my startled heart. I hence left the museum.
>
> 这是我到意大利的拿波里的第二天。吃了中饭独自走到国家考古博物院 […] 正在那里叹赏，忽然我的眼光被一种不知名的力吸引到一块残碎的 Fresco 上去。这块 Fresco 直不过二尺横不过一尺余，但是那画着的美妇却似乎用她的看情人的目光对吾说道：走向我处来吧，我的洵美！——啊，我醉了！我木了！我被诱惑了！我怎样走向她处去呢？走向她哪里去呢？走向她心里去吧，她的心是冷的。走向她灵魂里去吧，我自己的灵魂也怕早失掉了 […] 那看守者忽然和气起来，带着笑容对我用着意大利式的英文说："这是莎茀，希腊的女诗人。"

"啊原来她也是个诗人，可怕！可爱！"这是我受惊了的心灵颤抖出来了听不出的一句话。我于是便离去了博物院。¹

In early 1925 Shao arrived in Cambridge, attended a prep school and soon enrolled as a student of economics at Emmanuel College. He arranged a homestay with Arthur Christopher Moule, a sinologist and pastor who had once preached in China and was later one of the editors of *Marco Polo: The Description of the World* (1934).² As he settled down with Moule, his curiosity in Sappho again stirred. He recollects a sequence of actions triggered by this stirring curiosity:

> One day when arranging some books, I found a print of a Sappho fresco that I had bought in Rome. I hastily framed it and hung it in a place beside my book shelves. This print gave me some bizarre ideas, and my drafts overfilled with poems were piled up even higher. Then in a second-hand book store I bought an English translation of Sappho, in the foreword of which I read a story of how a group of archeologists excavated some papyruses carrying her poetry. This doubled my curiosity in the poetess. What she left us are fragments, among which "Hymn to Aphrodite" is the most complete; hereafter my most important task was to translate "Hymn to Aphrodite".

> 有一天为了要整理一些书籍，发现了一张在罗马买得的希腊壁画莎茀像的印刷品，连忙配了镜框把它挂在离我书架最近的地方。这画像又为我造出许多离奇的幻想，写满了诗句的草稿于是越积越多了。接着在一家旧书铺里又买到了一部莎茀诗的英译本，从序文里读到一班考古学家从沙漠里掘得她写在草叶上的诗歌的故事，使我对于这位女诗人发生了双倍的好奇心。她所遗留给我们的是些断篇的诗章，《爱神颂》是最完整的一首，从此我最重要的工作便是去译这首《爱神颂》了。³

---

¹ Shao, "Two Idols" (Liangge ouxiang 两个偶像), originally published in *La Maison D'Or Monthly* issue 5 (1929). Here quoted from *Rulin xinshi* 儒林新史 [A New History of Literati] (Shanghai: Shanghai shudian chubanshe, 2012), 6-7. "Rulin xinshi" was originally written as a series of articles published in the newspaper Xinbao 辛报, 18 June to 3 August, 1937. In 2012 an anthology of Shao's articles includes this series and uses the name as the book's title.

² A. C. Moule and Paul Pelliot, *Marco Polo: The Description of the World* (London: G. Routledge & Sons, Limited, 1938).

³ Shao, section 19 of "A New History of Literati", *A New History of Literati*, 98-99.

Shao spent a profusion of time on reading and attempting to translate into Chinese "Hymn to Aphrodite" and some other fragments of Sappho. But according to the three biographies of Shao, he had no training in Greek before he came to Cambridge. It might be assumed that Shao's translations of Sappho at this period were heavily dependent on Greek dictionaries and English translations. Shao writes in an article:

> When in Cambridge I laid aside for the sake of Sappho my study, which ought to be of utmost importance. I often forgot to eat or sleep; I rummaged through the Greek Lexicon to translate her poems into Chinese. Although the outcome was terrible, I found the comfort that I needed; I think at least I've used up all my energy to contribute what I could contribute.

> 我在剑桥的时候，竟为了 Sappho 而丢开了最紧要的功课，废寝忘食，翻了 Greek Lexicon 将她的诗译成中文，虽然译得不堪寓目，但是我自己已得到了我所需要的安慰；我觉得我至少已用了我所有的力量，来贡献了我所能贡献的一切。[4]

The outcome of this enthusiasm was manifest in *Roses and Roses*, a collection of translated poems Shao published in 1928, including "Hymn to Aphrodite" (Aishen song 爱神颂), the fragments Lobel 2[5] (Canshi yi 残诗一), Lobel 31 (Canshi er 残诗二), and Lobel 5 (Nüshen ge 女神歌). Besides his effort to translate Sappho into Chinese, Shao claims that he once wrote a short play based on the fragments of Sappho:

> There are about fifty, sixty fragments of Sappho that have been found, among which some fragments only have an incomplete sentence. In the spare time of my study I collaged them with my imagination and it turned out to become a short play. With the aid of Mr. Moule it was published by Heffers [...] This play is printed in an exquisite manner, with the hand-made paper bought from Cambridge University Press and the cover designed by British woodcut expert Eric Gill [...] But when this brochure appeared on the display table of Heffers, not even one copy was sold.

---

[4] Shao, "The Sorrow of Mochou" (Mochou zhichou 莫愁之愁), originally published in *Zhenshanmei* 真善美 volume 3, issue 5 (1929). Here quoted from *A Job that Can't Lie*, 11-12.
[5] This book uses Lobel-Page numbering to refer to Sappho's fragments.

莎茀诗被人发现的一共有五六十几个断片，有几个断片竟然只有一句不完全的话。我在正式的课程外，便把它们凭了自己的想象联系起来，结果写成了一出短剧。一由慕尔先生的介绍，交海法书店印刷发行 [...] 这册剧本印得特别讲究，纸张是剑桥大学出版部转买来的手造纸，封面的图样又是英国木刻名家吉尔先生的设计 [...] 但是当这本小册子出现在海法书店的陈列桌上以后，竟然一本也没有卖掉。6

That Sappho was back in vogue during the 20s might be the reason that triggered Shao's composition of the play.7 Many Sappho translations sprouted in the 20s, such as *The Poems of Sappho* by Edwin Marion Cox in 1924,8 *The Songs of Sappho* by David Moore Robinson and Marion Mills Miller in 1925.9

In 1929 Shao published an article entitled "Sappho the Greek Sage Poet" (as mentioned in the literature review section) and makes a précis of how the trend of Sappho recurs in Anglophone and Francophone literature. In the survey, Shao spends most ink on Baudelaire's "Lesbos". He writes: "Baudelaire prays in his poem 'Lesbos' that the sea could one day bring Sappho back to Lesbos [...] His poem is based on the story that Sappho kills herself for an unrequited love by jumping into the sea." ("鲍特莱尔在他的 Lesbos 一诗中，祈求着大海能有一晚将莎茀带回篮笥布 [...] 他这首诗是以莎茀因失恋而跳海的故事作题材的。")10 And he subsequently gives a quote with his own translation:

Car Lesbos entre tous m'a choisi sur la terre
Pour chanter le secret de ses vierges en fleurs

因为篮笥布从人世间挑选了个我
去为他们如花的处女的秘密唱歌11

The chosen one, he writes, is termed by Baudelaire as "la mâle Sapho, l'amante et le poète". Further he says: "What he calls la mâle Sapho, l'amante et le poète (the male Sappho, the lover and the poet) is Phaon, but also at the same time

---

6 Shao, *A New History of Literati*, 99.
7 The three biographies of Shao all affirm the existence of this book/brochure, but my attempt to locate/acquire it was unsuccessful. The validity of this account is still questionable.
8 Edwin Marion Cox, trans., *The Poems of Sappho* (London: Williams and Norgate, 1924).
9 David Moore Robinson and Marion Mills Miller, trans., *The Songs of Sappho* (New York: Frank-Maurice, 1925).
10 Shao, *Collected Works of Shao Xunmei*, 180.
11 Ibid.

Baudelaire himself [...] His admiration of Sappho has reached its vertex." ("他在诗中所指的 la mâle Sapho, l'amante et le poète! (男性的莎茀，情子与诗人！) 虽为飞虹 (Phaon)，但同时也便是他自己 [...] 他尊崇莎茀的心思实在热诚到极点了。")[12] Shao's admiration of Sappho also reached its vertex. He shares what he sees as Baudelaire's desire to be the "mâle Sapho", and sings for the secret of the virgin of Lesbos in his poem "To Sappho":[13]

> Your scent wakes from the bed made of flowers,
> Like a virgin's moon-like naked body—
> I can't see your skin that envelops fire and blood,
> But like roses you blossom in my heart.
>
> 你这从花床中醒来的香气，
> 也像那处女的明月般裸体—
> 我不见你包着火血的肌肤，
> 你却像玫瑰般开在我心里。[14]

Shao is yet to discover that around the bed made of flowers there is the third "mâle Sapho" singing for the virgin of Lesbos, who would leave a long-lasting influence on him.

1.1.2 From Sappho to Swinburne

After learning of Shao's obsession with Sappho, Moule introduced him to J. M. Edmonds, a renowned researcher on Greek classics in Jesus College, who translated and edited *Lyra Graeca: Being the Remains of All the Greek Lyric Poets from Eumelus to Timothes excepting Pindar* in 1922,[15] and later in 1928 published the anthology *Sappho Revocata*.[16] Shao includes in an article an excerpt of his diary that documents his first meeting with Edmonds:

> He said the loss of Sappho's three (?) poetry collections is a misfortune for literary scholars, and a misfortune for modern men [...] Then he said one could not see the real Sappho in translations and that the color and

---

[12] Ibid.
[13] The original title is in English.
[14] Originally published in *Tusu* 屠苏 August issue (1926). Here quoted from *Poetic Works of Shao Xunmei*, 20.
[15] J. M. Edmonds, *Lyra Graeca: Being the Remains of All the Greek Lyric Poets from Eumelus to Timothes excepting Pindar* (London: W. Heinemann, 1922).
[16] J. M. Edmonds, *Sappho Revocata* (London: Peter Davies, 1928).

music of the originals could only be felt in the originals [...] In the end he said if I want to feel the beauty of Sappho before I could comprehend her original poems, I should read Swinburne's poems, and that there is a piece in *Poems and Ballads* that is the most successful application of Sapphic meter in modern English poetry.

> 他说：莎茀的三本(?)诗集的遗失，实在是文学界的不幸，现代人的不幸[...] 他又说：在译文中决不能见到莎茀于万一，原诗的色彩与音乐只能在原诗中去领略 [...] 末了他又说：假使我在未能读莎茀原诗以前而欲领略一些莎茀的美，我可以去读史文朋的诗，史文朋在他的诗歌集第一卷中的一首，是现代作家中用莎茀诗格写英文诗的最成功的一首。[17]

Note that in the reported speech of Edmonds the phrase of "color and music" is used to describe the quality of Sappho's original poems. Though Shao might not seem to realize his interest in the condition of music in poetry at this stage in Cambridge, it could be deduced that this phrase or what this phrase paraphrases is so memorable to Shao that it features in this recollection. Shao then recalls in the article: "What makes me still grateful to him is that at that time he let me come to know the name of Swinburne. The next morning I bought a copy of *Poems and Ballads*. After just a flip through the pages, immediately, a quarter of my heart was seized by him, just as by Sappho." ("尤其使我现在还感激他的，便是他同时使我知道了史文朋的名字。翌日的早晨我便去买了一本史文朋的诗歌集第一卷，仅仅翻来一看，我的心立刻又被他像莎茀般地占去了四分之一。")[18]

Here, Shao, Sappho and Swinburne are eventually gathered. In "Sappho the Greek Sage Poet" Shao quotes a sentence from W. L. Courtney[19]: "Shelley has the true lyrical note, and Keats some of that chiselled loveliness which makes each Sapphic stanza a masterpiece." ("雪莱得到了她的抒情的调子，济慈则得到了她的那种使每句句子均成绝响的雕刻美。")[20] It is interesting to know the sentences that immediately precede and follow this verdict in Courtney's very article, which are as follows:

> There are, perhaps, only two modern English poets who come anywhere near Sappho, or perhaps three, despite the number of those who have

---

[17] Shao, "Two Idols", *A New History of Literati*, 9.
[18] Ibid.
[19] William Leonard Courtney (1850-1928) was a British author and literary critic.
[20] Shao, *Collected Works of Shao Xunmei*, 182.

tried to imitate her [...] And then, last of all, and in some ways best of all, we come, not to Rossetti, but to Swinburne.[21]

In a similar fashion, Shao ends his survey of the recurrence of Sappho as a literary trend by placing Swinburne at the very end of the long chain of English literature: "But in England the one who admires Sappho the most is Swinburne. Here I would borrow a phrase from Baudelaire to call him la mâle Sapho." ("但在英格兰最崇拜莎茀的人是史文朋。我在这里也要借用鲍特莱尔的句子喊他一声 la mâle Sapho 了。")[22] Another interesting parallel is that Courtney in his article quotes lines from Swinburne's "Anactoria" in which he ventriloquizes as Sappho to address her lover Anactoria, while Shao in his article goes on to applaud the very same poem by saying: "The poem with its surging ideas, flowing poeticality and copious music, describes the joy in sorrow, the pity in ire and the longing in despair; I think even if Sappho could write it herself, it wouldn't be more blazing and bright." ("全篇以滔滔的思想，源源的诗意，洋洋的音乐，来形容苦恼中之快乐，忿怒中之爱怜，绝望中之欲求；我想即使莎茀自己来写，也不过这样炽烈与灿烂了。")[23] Based on these two sets of resemblance, it could be assumed that beside Edmonds' recommendation, Shao's laudation of Swinburne might be much influenced by Courtney. The difference is that Courtney's applause for Swinburne remains a critical assessment while Shao's laudation morphs into an enthusiasm. Note the phrase of "copious music" in the laudation, which resonates with "color and music" in the indirect speech of Edmonds. One could deduce that the condition of music has been associated with Sappho and Swinburne from the early stage of Shao's life, where he came to know the works of the two poets. In the article Shao quotes from "A Singer Asleep", Hardy's elegy for Swinburne, along with his own translation:

> "O teacher, where lies hid thy burning line;
> Where are those songs, O poetess divine,
> Whose very arts are love incarnadine?"
> And her smile back: "Disciple true and warm,
> Sufficient now are thine."

---

[21] W. L. Courtney, *Old Saws and Modern Instances* (London: Forgotten Books, 2013), *96*.
[22] Shao, *Collected Works of Shao Xunmei*, 181-182.
[23] Shao, *Collected Works of Shao Xunmei*, 182-183.

"啊先生，你的火炽的句子在哪里；
你的歌曲在哪里，啊，神圣的诗人，
你残弃的遗物何非肉色的爱情？"
于是她回了一笑："热诚的信徒吓，
你自己的已经尽够了。"²⁴

Shao's selection of this poem and this excerpt is certainly not random. Here Swinburne is remembered as a "singer", and the lines quoted feature the word of "songs", both of which pertain to music. The teacher here refers to Sappho. By quoting these lines, Shao seems to imply that Swinburne, the disciple of Sappho, has equally "incarnadine" arts and "sufficient" songs. Though the poetry of Swinburne was at the beginning a temporary expedient when Shao lacked the competence in ancient Greek to comprehend Sappho's original poems, it turns out that Shao's admiration of Sappho was gradually outweighed by his admiration of Swinburne. That being said, Sappho never left the horizon of Shao during his literary career. She continues to be, as an incarnation of poetry, in every nightingale that sings.

1.1.3 A poet in the making

After coming to know the works of Swinburne, Shao admits that his interest in the study of economics greatly lessens and that he "could no longer focus on books to which I should've paid more attention" ("心思再也不能回复到原有的书籍上").²⁵ He writes:

> Afternoons in the library, I only wandered around the shelves of poetry. Every day from the window of my flat I saw the apple trees on the lawn; I saw the gravestones of the church next door. I almost felt that I could touch the truth if I reach out my hands, and faintly I felt the urge to change my subject of study. Every piece of non-important thing would lead me into my memory, and so I called to mind the joy neglected and bliss ignored in the past. All the thoughts that hovered in my head, were by me rendered into lines that rhyme; I even fooled myself into a belief that I'm a poet that people anticipate.

---

²⁴ Hardy's "A Singer Asleep" VIII. Here quoted from *Collected Works of Shao Xunmei*, 182.
²⁵ Shao, *A New History of Literati*, 98.

下午在图书馆里，也只是在诗歌的架子边上徘徊，每天从寝室的窗口，看到了草地里的苹果树，看到了隔壁礼拜堂后面的墓碑，我似乎感觉到一伸手便可以触到真理，又隐隐地明白我有改行的必要。每一样不重要的事都会把我领进回忆里，我于是追怀着过去所忽略的愉快，和没有重视的幸福。这种萦绕心头的思虑，我全把来写成压了脚韵的句子；自己竟然相信自己是一个大家所等待着的诗人了。26

These "lines that rhyme" were not published until 1926, in the August issue of *Tusu* (屠苏), a journal edited by the Sphinx Club. Shao published three poems entitled "To Swinburne", "To Sappho",27 "Horror" (Kongbu 恐怖) and a translation of Swinburne's "A Match" (Pi'ou 匹偶). This was one of the earliest publishing attempts of Shao and the outcome was applauded by Chai Shuduo 柴树铎28 as "full of music, colors, emotion and power" ("有声，有色，有情，有力").29 Note the occurrence of "music" here. The diction as such is not unusual in the criticism of Shao. These three poems eventually culminated in *Heaven and May*, Shao's first poetry collection. The advertisement for this collection appears in *La Maison D'Or Monthly* as follows:

> His poems are deft, charming, pungent, coquettish, appetizing; and yet frantic, dauntless—he says everything, everything that people dare not say. Each and every piece is a scented corolla of soul that is full of the breath of spring, the sweetness of flesh and the magnificent magic that seduces all. His poetic realm is worth our appreciation, marvel and drunkenness.
>
> 他的诗格是轻灵的、娇媚的、浓腻的、妖艳的、香喷的；而又狂纵的，大胆的—什么都说出来，人家所不能说不敢道的。简直首首都是香迷心窍的灵葩，充满着春的气息，肉的甜香，包含着诱惑一切的伟大魔力。真值得我们欣赏、赞叹，沉醉在他的诗境里边。30

Shao's poetic career is thus launched, but his passion for translating and introducing Swinburne to Chinese readers did not cease here. In 1928 he

---

26 Ibid.
27 The original titles of these two poems are in English.
28 An author and literary critic in Republican China.
29 "Tusu" (屠苏), originally published in *Beixin* (北新) issue 10 (23 Oct 1926); here quoted from *A Selection of Works and Critical Reception of Sphinx Club*, 260.
30 An interleaf advertisement in *La Maison D'Or Monthly* volume 1, issue 2 (1 February 1929).

published *Roses and Roses*, a collection of translated poems in which he anthologizes four translations of Swinburne, "Song" (Ge 歌), "Before Dawn" (Riluo zhiqian 日落之前), "The Oblation" (Gongfeng 供奉) and "A Match" (Pi'ou 匹偶). In the same year he published *Fire and Flesh* (Huo yu rou 火与肉), an anthology of critical essays. In the dedication Shao cites "Hands that sting like fire" from Swinburne's "Before Dawn", and the anthology features two essays on Swinburne: "Swinburne" (Shiwenpeng 史文朋) and "Songs before Sunrise" (Richuqian zhi ge 日出前之歌).

1928 witnessed a creative explosion from Shao. Beside *Roses and Roses* and *Fire and Flesh*, in this year, he published his second poetry collection *Flower-like Evil*, the title of which pays an overt tribute to *Les Fleurs du Mal*. This collection shows the poetic caliber of Shao and was much acclaimed by the critics. Shen Congwen 沈从文 comments on *Flower-like Evil*: "Shao Xunmei composes his poetry collection in a way that resembles a hymn to the senses. Hymning life, hymning love; there emerges the hedonism of an aesthete, the exaggerated clinging to the earthly world yet in such a world he still sees a void." ("邵询美以官能的颂歌那样感情写成他的诗集。赞美生, 赞美爱, 然而显出唯美派人生的享乐, 对于现世的夸张的贪恋, 对于现世又仍然看到空虚。")[31] It should be noted that here Shen uses the word "hymn" (Songge 颂歌), a word that pertains to music to describe Shao's poetry. There must be something in Shao's poetry that triggers Shen's word choice, though in the passage, he does not elaborate on his diction. Interestingly, Shen's comment is reminiscent of Shao's own applause of Swinburne and Baudelaire as he regards them as "creators and patron saints of all the poetry of truth, beauty, love, music and sweetness" ("他俩是创造主, 是一切真的、美的、情的、音乐的、甜蜜的诗歌的爱护神") and claims that "their poetry always finds fragrance from stench, truth from falsehood, goodness from evil, beauty from ugliness, diversion from life's depression, happiness from a world of melancholy" ("他俩的诗都是在臭中求香; 在假中求真; 在恶中求善; 在丑中求美; 在苦闷的人生中求兴趣; 在忧愁的世界中求快活").[32] Here Shao uses a phrase "patron saints of all the poetry of [...] music" to express his adoration for Swinburne. In fact, words that pertain to music are

---

[31] Shen Congwen, "How Do We Read New Poetry" (Women zenmeyang qudu xinshi 我们怎么样去读新诗), originally published in Xiandai xuesheng 现代学生 [Modern Student] issue 1 (1930); here quoted from Zhongguo xiandai shilun 中国现代诗论 上 [*Modern Chinese Poetics Volume* 1], ed. Yang Kuanghan 杨匡汉 (Guangzhou: Huacheng chubanshe, 1985), 136.
[32] Shao, *Fire and Flesh*, 20; translated by Leo Lee in *Shanghai Modern: The Flowering of a New Urban Culture in China*, 248.

everywhere to be found in his critical works. This kind of word most frequently appears in his criticism on Swinburne, such as his essay "Swinburne" in *Fire and Flesh* which describes the poetry of Swinburne as consisting of "words like pearls immersed in music" ("浸在音乐中的珍珠般美的字儿").[33]

Beside the applause from Shao, Swinburne has often been critiqued with words that pertain to music. He was once described by Tennyson as "a reed through which all things blow into music"[34] and in Hardy's lament "[...] a minstrel who/ Blew them [fresh-fluted notes] not naively, but as one who knew/ Full well why thus he blew".[35] Swinburne himself also has a tendency to use words that pertain to music in poetry criticism, as Thomas E. Connolly observes:

> More than any other critic of his day, Algernon Charles Swinburne judged poetry by its music, but, because Swinburne is so often ignored as a critic, much of what he had to say on this most elusive subject remains buried in his involved critical prose.[36]

Shao and Swinburne both tend to "judge poetry by its music" and are both frequently judged in terms of the music of their poetry. To shed light on how Swinburne's idea of music might have influenced Shao's, and to make this "most elusive subject" less elusive, a survey of Swinburne's use of words that pertain to music will be necessary.

1.2 Harmony as a condition of music in poetry

1.2.1 Swinburne's conception of harmony

Jerome McGann observes that harmony might be a key term in Swinburne's discussion of the music of poetry:

> Poetry, he writes, has only "one final and irreplaceable requisite": "inner harmony" ("Emily Bronte," *Works*, 14:46). The point is insistent even when Swinburne discusses a poet like Wordsworth, so dear to Arnold's moral program: though "rare, uncertain, [and] intermittent" in his verse, "though unable to command his music at will with the assurance of a

---

[33] Shao, *Fire and Flesh*, 26.
[34] Here quoted from John D. Rosenberg, "Swinburne", *Victorian Studies* 11, no. 2 (1967): 152.
[35] Quoted from Philip Henderson, *Swinburne: The Portrait of a Poet* (London: Routledge & Kegan Paul, 1974), 285.
[36] Thomas E. Connolly, "Swinburne on 'The Music of Poetry'", *PMLA* 72, no. 4 (1957): 680.

Milton or a Shelley," nonetheless Wordsworth is a great poet when he achieves what poetry requires - "profound and majestic harmony" ("Wordsworth and Byron," *Works*, 14:240).[37]

McGann claims that in Swinburne's notion "inner harmony" is the "one final and irreplaceable requisite" for poetry. However, the quote from "Emily Brontë" is rather displaced for it comes from a context where Swinburne is making a comparison between *Mehalah*[38] and *Wuthering Heights*:

> But the accumulated horrors of the close [of *Mehalah*], however possible in fact, are wanting in the one quality which justifies and ennobles all admissible horror in fiction: they hardly seem inevitable; they lack the impression of logical and moral certitude. All the realism in the world will not suffice to convey this impression; and a work of art which wants it wants the one final and irreplaceable requisite of inner harmony.[39]

From the original text, one can see that "inner harmony" is not in Swinburne's notion the requisite for poetry as McGann observes, but a requisite for "the impression of logical and moral certitude" in any work of art. Though this quote from "Emily Brontë" is clearly abused, McGann does make a point with the quote regarding Wordsworth. Swinburne does use the phrase "profound and majestic harmony" when it comes to the poetry of Wordsworth. McGann writes:

> This "harmony" is the meaning of all poems [...] The thought seems simple enough, perhaps even banal. But much more is involved here than a Romantic formalism akin to Coleridge's famous idea of poetry as "the balance or reconciliation of opposite or discordant qualities." When Swinburne speaks of a poem's harmony, his thought is always tied to a set of musical ideas and analogies. The significance of that relationship, though well known, has scarcely begun to be understood or appreciated.[40]

---

[37] Jerome McGann, "Wagner, Baudelaire, Swinburne: Poetry in the Condition of Music", *Victorian Poetry* 47, no. 4, "A hundred sleeping years ago": In commemoration of Algernon Charles Swinburne, 2009: 621.
[38] S. Baring-Gould, *Mehalah, A Story of the Salt Marshes* (London: Smith, Elder and Co, 1880).
[39] Originally published in *Athenaeum*, June 1883; here quoted from *The Brontës: The Critical Heritage,* ed. Miriam Farris Allott (London: Psychology Press, 1974), 439.
[40] McGann, "Wagner, Baudelaire, Swinburne: Poetry in the Condition of Music", 621.

Here McGann claims that "this 'harmony' is the meaning of all poems". The validity of this statement will be examined later. What seems valid at this point is McGann's observation that this notion of harmony is "tied to a set of musical ideas and analogies". As Swinburne in his criticism on Wordsworth does use phrases like "command his music" to accompany "profound and majestic harmony", it is true that what Swinburne terms as harmony could not be simply equated with congruity. Connolly also affirms that harmony is an important word in "Swinburne's critical vocabulary of the music of poetry".[41] The significance of the relationship between this notion of harmony and the music of poetry, as McGann points out, is in need of further investigation.

As Swinburne's critical works are often diffuse and nowhere near systematic, any attempt to locate a definite definition for his coined terms would often end up in failure. One way to circumvent this might be to carefully collect and put together related puzzle pieces that are scattered over various articles in his critical corpus. Swinburne's notion of harmony could not be studied alone and must be read against his other notions on the music of poetry. Notably, Swinburne applauds Shelley's "singing" ability in this manner:

> Shelley outsang all poets on record but some two or three throughout all time; his depths and heights of inner and outer music are as divine as nature's and not sooner exhaustible. He was alone the perfect singing-god; his thoughts, words, deeds, all sang together." [42]

It should be noted that here Swinburne comes up with two interesting terms: inner and outer music. The definitions are not given in the context, neither is any elaboration on this topic in the subsequent text. Charles E. Russell observes:

> In all his practice, words have two functions as the media of poetic art. They have, first, their definitive use, as the symbols of ideas, by which thought is conveyed, design and purpose established, structure is built, imagery and figurework are added; and they have, second, but hardly inferior, certain distinct and multifold tone values, which, in his method, are woven into carefully wrought-out schemes of sound intended to

---

[41] Connolly, "Swinburne on 'The Music of Poetry'", 685.
[42] Swinburne, "Notes on the Text of Shelley", *Essays and Studies* (London: Chatto and Windus, 1875), 215.

emphasize, clarify, vivify the feeling conveyed by the definitive function or bare meaning of the words.[43]

In Russell's opinion, the first function, the "definitive use" of words might be what Swinburne calls inner music while the second function, the acoustic features of a poem, might be in line with Swinburne's notion of outer music. Is this interpretation correct?

Swinburne writes in the monograph *William Blake. A Critical Essay*: "The sound of many verses of Blake's cleaves to the sense long after conscious thought of the meaning has passed from one: a sound like running of water or ringing of bells in a long lull of the wind."[44] Here Swinburne enunciates a pair of entities that could be the interpretations of inner and outer music respectively: meaning and sound. Judging from this excerpt, one could confirm the previous conjecture that Swinburne's notion of inner music could be equated with meaning or sense, while outer music could be equated with the sound or the acoustic aspect of a poem. What should be noted is that the sound that "cleaves to the sense", namely the sound of the verses of Blake which Swinburne applauds, is compared to the natural sound of running water and bells ringing by the wind. And if one goes back to the previous excerpt on Shelley, one will see a comparison of Shelley's inner and outer music with those of nature ("his depths and heights of inner and outer music are as divine as nature's"). What he seems to suggest might be that the union of sound and meaning is most solid when it resembles things in nature. He writes later in the book: "The Piper, the Lamb, the Chimney-sweeper, and the two-days-old baby ["Infant Joy"]; all, for the music in them, more like the notes of birds caught up and given back than the modulated measure of human verse." [45] Here Swinburne prefers the notes of the birds, a symbol of nature, to "the modulated measure of human verse". From these three excerpts, one can deduce that Swinburne considers nature as the ideal, perfect paradigm for the merging of inner and outer music in poetry, which could be interpreted as a union of meaning and sound. This merging of inner and outer music is in his notion a condition where poetry is musical.

Now let us bring back his notion of harmony. What is the relationship between harmony and nature, Swinburne's perfect paradigm for the merging of inner and outer music? Connolly's observation is interesting:

---

[43] Charles E. Russell, "Swinburne and Music", *The North American Review* 186, no. 624 (1907): 429.
[44] Swinburne, *William Blake. A Critical Essay* (London: John Camden Hotten, 1868), 10.
[45] Ibid., 115-116.

> Harmony is a term that goes beyond either 'external' or 'inner' music [...] When 'external' and 'inner' music blend, the result is harmony [...] It is the word in which the other words such as imagination, passion, external music, and inner music find their resolution and their proper meaning.[46]

If one agrees on the notion that the result of the blending of inner and outer music is harmony, one could say that harmony is the condition where poetry is musical and that nature would be the perfect paradigm for harmony. Notably, T. S. Eliot in "Swinburne as Poet" makes a famous verdict that "in Swinburne the meaning and the sound are one thing".[47] The phrase "one thing" denotes a perfect union of meaning and sound, the merging of inner and outer music as Swinburne puts it. In this sense, the "one thing" that Eliot does not further scrutinize might be the condition of harmony that Swinburne aspires to achieve in poetry.

After piecing up a possible interpretation of Swinburne's notion of harmony with puzzle pieces collected from his critical works, it would be helpful to see if this interpretation could be applied to his poetic practices. Swinburne's poetry is full of symbols. As seen from his critique on Blake, birds are often chosen by Swinburne to be the sound-making symbol for nature and to illustrate his notion of harmony in poetry. This is evident in his poem "A Match":

> If I were what the words are,
> And love were like the tune,
> With double sound and single
> Delight our lips would mingle,
> With kisses glad as birds are
> That get sweet rain at noon;
> If I were what the words are,
> And love were like the tune.[48]

The matching of "the tune" and "the words" is compared to birds "that get sweet rain at noon". "The tune", the acoustic features, denote what Swinburne considers as the outer music of a poem while "the words" refer to the meaning of the poem and hence correspond with his notion of inner music. "The tune"

---

[46] Connolly, "Swinburne on 'The Music of Poetry'", 685.
[47] T. S. Eliot, "Swinburne as Poet", *The Sacred Wood: Essays on Poetry and Criticism*, ed. T. S. Eliot (New York: Alfred A. Knopf, 1921), 135.
[48] A. C. Swinburne, *Poems and Ballads*, 116.

and "the words" are a match in the symbol of bird, and so is the union of sound and meaning, the merging of outer and inner music.

Shao translated this poem as *Pi'ou* 匹偶 and published it in the August issue of *Tusu* in 1926, the year in which he returned from Cambridge. One could deduce that he must have read the poem during his education in England. Two years later, this poem was anthologized in his collection of translated poems, *Roses and Roses*. This gives us another hint that he thinks highly of this poem. These clues confirm that this poem had an influence on Shao. It is unknown whether Shao read the previously cited excerpts on Wordsworth, Shelley and Blake, but what is known is that in Shao's oeuvre one could see a similar preference for the symbol of the bird, as evident in poems like "A Sonnet" (Shisihang shi 十四行诗), "Tomorrow" (Mingtian 明天), "Divine Light" (Shenguang 神光) and "Flower" (Hua 花):

> The scarce leaves of the tree of life,
> Twenty-one pieces have been plucked by time.
> The bird that hides in a nest among branches,
> Was yet to try out his gifted feathers;
> He used to fiddle with his tender voice,
> But a dirty and massive curtain of fog,
> Keeps the one behind from hearing.

> 生命之树底稀少的叶子，
> 被时光摘去二十一片了。
> 躲藏在枝间巢中的小鸟，
> 还没试用他天赐的羽翼；
> 他曾低弄他细嫩的喉音，
> 但有污浊而坚厚的雾幕，
> 挡住着幕中人不能听得。[49]

> How unexpected, this yellow flower blossoms,
> Everything blossoms,
> On the pavement of air,
> Flying birds come and go.

---

[49] "A Sonnet" (Shisihang shi 十四行诗), *Poetic Works of Shao Xunmei*, 94.

这朵黄花竟然开了，
一切都开了，
空气的道上，
复忙着来往的行鸟。 50

Weeping its unnamed laughter,
Flowers and birds once in the same garden;
The withered are withered, the dead are dead,
The unwithered undead tonight has come.

是悲泣是不知名的欢笑，
原是同一园中的花与鸟；
谢的谢了死的也死了，
不谢不死的今夜来到。 51

He's most scared of the sad songbird,
Grumbling in the sweet honeyed air;
A tune that should've been happy,
Is but piped with tears.

他最怕那悲哀的鸣鸟，
在甜蜜的空中说牢骚；
明明是快乐的歌调，
却含着眼泪来呼号。 52

Though the bird is a recurring symbol in the poetry of Shao, not all the birds simply appear with a general name as "bird". In a poem entitled "Nature's Order" (Ziran de mingling 自然的命令) one could see that Shao deploys bird symbols of various specific species or even from mythologies:

Nature's order, the power to choose is hers.
As long as she will, she could place her heart
Between the wings of Dapeng[53] in the azure flying,
She could follow the hawk with the quickest eyes
To shoot that unrelaxing arrow; she could also

---

[50] "Tomorrow" (Mingtian 明天), *Poetic Works of Shao Xunmei*, 104.
[51] "Divine Light" (Shenguang 神光), *Poetic Works of Shao Xunmei*, 192.
[52] "Flower" (Hua 花), *Poetic Works of Shao Xunmei*, 24-25.
[53] A giant bird that metamorphoses from a huge fish in Chinese mythology.

Let pigeons take her to a steady ride, ride
To the apex of clouds, and oversee with pride
Flock of friends that used to chase her madly.

自然的命令，选择的权柄是她的。
只要她愿意，她可以安置她的心
在大鹏鸟的翅膀中间飞上青天，
她也可以跟随最眼快的老鹰
射那不肯放松的一箭; 她也可以
让白鸽带了她平稳地旅行，旅行
到顶高的云端，再骄傲地俯瞰
那一群曾疯癫地追逐她的朋友。54

[…]
You can tell the vain Fenghuang[55]
That you have thousands of peonies, that you have
A sun for her to groom against from morn to dawn;
You can tell the fierce raven that you have
A bed three hundred times softer than a magpie nest:
Suffering is their status, God grants you.
But you shouldn't lie to her, you should
Let her enjoy the twice caressing of spring breeze,
So she would know this huge cosmos never
Treats her badly, never gets bored of her songs.

[…]
你可以对虚荣的凤凰
说你有几千几万朵牡丹，说你有
一面太阳可以早晚照着她梳装;
你可以对强悍的乌鸦说你有比
喜鹊的窝巢三百倍温软的床铺:
苦楚是他们的名分，上帝许你。
可是你总不应当骗她，你得让
她尽量地享受两次春风的抚拂，

---

[54] Shao, *Poetic Works of Shao Xunmei*, 142.
[55] An immortal bird in Chinese mythology that bears some similarities to the phoenix.

让她明白这老大的宇宙从没有
待亏她，从没有厌倦她的吟咏。 56

However, the high flying of Dapeng, the quick eyes of hawks, the steadiness of pigeons, or Fenghuang's sun as a grooming mirror are ultimately of little signification when compared to songs that could last forever in the cosmos. For Shao, the bird that is capable of everlasting songs is the nightingale. The nightingale takes an unsurpassable lead in frequency among all the birds whose species are clearly identified in his works. This is also evident in the oeuvre of Swinburne. What I will venture to do in the next section is to examine the use of the symbol of the nightingale in Swinburne's and Shao's works to see if the conception of harmony migrates, like a bird, from Swinburne to Shao.

1.2.2 The nightingale as a symbol of harmony

Swinburne's obsession with the nightingale can date back to a poem entitled "The Nightingale", which according to the observation of Georges Lafourcade might be written during Swinburne's college days in Oxford:[57]

> Thro' the thick throbbings of her trembling throat,
> Half stifled with its music, struggling gush'd
> The torrent-tide of song, then free burst out
> And in a tempest whirl of melody rush'd
> Thro' the stirred boughs. The young leaves on the trees
> Flutter'd, as in a storm, to that harmonious breeze.
> It floated now serenely, sweet of breath,
> As with full conscious beauty now content,
> Now shivered into dim delicious death,
> Dash'd down a precipice of music, rent
> By the mad stream of song whirl'd, shook, rang out, spoke,
> Stunning the charmed night with long melodies,
> Then in a thousand gurgling eddies flew
> Of whirlwind sweetness, lost in its own sound,[58]

The progression of the singing of the nightingale is illustrated with verbs of motion: "gush'd", "rush'd", "floated", "shivered" and "dash'd down". The singing of the nightingale is described with an attempt to re-present the significance

---

[56] Shao, *Poetic Works of Shao Xunmei*, 144.
[57] Georges Lafourcade, *Swinburne's Hyperion and Other Poems with an Essay on Swinburne and Keats* (London: Faber & Gwyer, 1927), 147.
[58] Ibid., 149.

perceived when hearing the nightingale sing. In this way, the outer music, the sound of the nightingale is merged with the description of the changes of motion, the inner music of the poem. The outer and inner music are merged in the symbol of the nightingale and form a condition of harmony. According to Lafourcade's observation, this was written by a young Swinburne who was yet to begin his poetic career. But what seems certain from this early poem is his interest in the music of poetry and his use of the nightingale as a symbol for the union of meaning and sound, which evolved in his later career as an idea that is termed as harmony, or the merging of inner and outer music as he puts it.

Interestingly, Shao's obsession with the nightingale could also date back to as early as his compositions in Cambridge, such as "Sister Flower" (Huazizi 花姊姊) that is later anthologized in *Heaven and May*.

> Nature's mysteries cannot be uncorked,
> The abstruseness of buddha is not to be clarified,
> The cunning of the demiurge (malicious)
> Can but exist unresolved
> In the heart of commoners.
> […]
> She doesn't get it,
> The one who gets it
> Is a nightingale that moans.
>
> 天机的秘密不可泄漏，
> 佛法的玄妙万难道明，
> 造物的狡狯（恶毒）
> 只能也不解而存在
> 凡人的内心。
> […]
> 她没懂得，
> 懂的是那
> 哀叫的一只夜莺。[59]

To comprehend this poem, let us bring in an article by Shao entitled "Nightingale" (Yeying 夜莺) published in 1930, in which he admits that he has "never heard a nightingale sing" and hence for him "it is a misty dreamy idea, a kind of music only enjoyed by gods; I could only imagine, envy and sense it

---

[59] Shao, *Poetic Works of Shao Xunmei*, 77-78.

from others' works". ("我是从来没有听得过夜莺的，因此于我这是一种缥缈的梦思，一种神仙的歌乐；我只有去幻想，去羡慕，去从人家的诗文里意会了。")[60] The sound of a nightingale is to him "a misty dreamy idea", which could be paraphrased as this: the sound is to him an idea, and the idea is misty as well as dreamy. It should be noted that "the sound is an idea" is actually a hint of the union of meaning and sound, the merging of inner and outer music as Swinburne proposes. Shao then describes this "misty dreamy idea" as "a kind of music only enjoyed by gods". By linking this idea with music, Shao indicates that the union of sound and meaning will result in a condition which he calls music. This condition of music is what Swinburne terms as the state of harmony.

As Shao sees it, this music is "only enjoyed by gods", and gods could take so many forms as illustrated in the previously cited "Sister Flower", such as Buddha and the demiurge. One should note that in the excerpt, Buddha and the demiurge are juxtaposed with nature. Gods in different names are to Shao various forms of nature. He writes in the poem that the commoners cannot get the mysteries of nature, but a nightingale does. Here the role of the nightingale is the same as the birds in Swinburne's "A Match", which I have discussed earlier. Shao sees the nightingale as the ideal symbol of nature. As he considers nature as the perfect paradigm for the condition of harmony, or the merging of inner and outer music as Swinburne puts it, he regards the nightingale as the perfect embodiment for the condition of harmony. On these two points, Shao and Swinburne are identical.

Let us get back to the excerpt from "Nightingale". Shao states that he could only "imagine, envy and sense" the sound of a nightingale from "others' works". These "other's works" might very likely include "Keats' Ode to a Nightingale" (Jici de yeyingge 济慈的夜莺歌), an article written by Xu Zhimo 徐志摩, one of the most celebrated Chinese modern poets. Shao writes: "In China, Zhimo held a splendid fiesta so everyone erects a memorial tablet in their mind for this 'infatuating bird' whose 'voice gets louder and louder, tune fancier and fancier, emotion hotter and hotter, charm lingering and lingering, like endless delight, flamboyant adoration, or modified sorrow'." ("在中国，志摩来了个伟艳的祭典，什么人的心中于是都供奉着这一只唱得 '声音越来越响亮，调门越来越新奇，情绪越来越热烈，韵味越来越深长，像是无限的欢畅，像是艳丽的怨慕，又像是变调的悲哀' 的 '发痴的鸟'。")[61] As Xu claims that he could hear a

---

[60] Shao, *A Job that Can't Lie*, 21.
[61] Shao, "Nightingale", *A Job that Can't Lie*, 21.

nightingale from the window of his flat,[62] Shao narrates a story of how he once attempted to hear the singing of a nightingale by staying in Xu's place:

> After two days of visiting I still hadn't heard the sound of a nightingale. I almost suspected that what Zhimo had heard was but the illusion of a poet, a dream, a poem of his own […] Back at home, I sat by my desk and turned on my green-shaded lamp, trying to imagine the tune of a nightingale. The books by my hands all laughed at me. They laughed at me for I don't know that poetry is as mysterious as nature; you can only comprehend, not explain; you can only appreciate, not imitate.

> 就这般地连续去了两天，却没曾听得夜莺。我几乎要怀疑志摩他所听得的不过是诗人的幻象，是梦，是他自己的诗 […] 回家，坐在书桌旁，开了我那绿罩子的台灯，想去理想出个夜莺的调子。手边的书本都对我笑了。他笑我不知道自然的一切和诗是同样的神秘，你只能去领会，不能去解释；你只能去欣赏，不能去模仿。[63]

In the passage Shao goes on to quote "A Third Thing" from D. H. Lawrence:

> Water is H2O, hydrogen two parts, oxygen one,
> But there is also a third thing, that makes it water
> And nobody knows what it is.
> The atom locks up two energies
> But it is a third thing present which makes it an atom.[64]

He writes: "To know this is to know everything. I hence gave up the idea to imagine the tune of a nightingale and fell asleep on the desk." ("领悟了这个便领悟了一切。我于是放弃了去理想夜莺的调子的念头，伏在书桌上睡了。")[65] What is known by Shao here is not explicitly explained to the readers. Shao never intends to create a theory in a systematic way. He puts forth a notion in the excerpt that "poetry is as mysterious as nature", which again resonates with Swinburne's applause for nature as the perfect paradigm for poetry. The thing that makes hydrogen and oxygen water is exactly the mysterious nature which makes inner and outer music blend in the symbol of the nightingale. Notably,

---

[62] This account is questionable as nightingales are only native to Europe and south-west Asia.
[63] Shao, *A Job that Can't Lie*, 22.
[64] Ibid., 23.
[65] Ibid., 23.

Shao claims that he later wakes up to what he perceives to be the singing of a nightingale:

> There are first some twitters, soft and gentle, like swift tender fingers testing the strings. Then come a few minutes of silence. Is she refining her powder? Is she adjusting her clothes? There begins a light and soothing honey-englobed whisper, as if it brings a sweet scent that a mouth exudes, not intense, but enough to make a heart sour and a soul drunk. What follows is the account of her long-hidden stories: she remembers she's a naive virgin; she remembers she's a picked flower, a queen in bed; she remembers she's a blissful goddess; she remembers she's a jealous girl, a lustful married woman, a tainted soul, a tattered scar, an abandoned fragment. She also remembers she's a spring that returns, a peony that re-blossoms, a self retrieved.

> 最先是温柔又细弱的几声，像是灵活的纤指在试弦。接着是几分钟的沉默。是在添粉？是在整衣？再开始是轻又小的含蜜的软语，似乎带来了口露的香气，不浓，却尽够将心来酸透，魂来醉倒。跟着来的是她心事的说诉：她记得她是个天真的处女；她记得她是个被折了的花朵，她记得她是个床上的皇后；她记得她是个美满的神仙；她记得她是个妒忌的女子；她记得她是个风流的少妇；她记得她是个染污的灵魂；她记得她是个碎痛的创痕；她记得她是个遗弃了的残片。她更记得她是个重来的新春，再开的牡丹，收回来了的自己。[66]

Note that the nightingale here is gendered. It is rendered by Shao a female while it is usually a male nightingale that sings. This is a practice similar to that used by Swinburne in "The Nightingale", which I have discussed earlier. Moreover, the phrases "refining her powder" and "adjusting her clothes" cue a metaphor that cleaves the nightingale to a woman. This woman could concurrently metamorphose into various beings: virgin, flower, queen, goddess, scar, fragment. Although these beings are concurrent, they do not conflict with each other as they are harmonious in the significance of the nightingale-woman. In this sense, the nightingale-woman is the symbol for harmony.

This nightingale-woman is somewhat familiar. The link of the nightingale-woman to "an abandoned fragment" seems to cue Sappho and her one-line fragment "spring's messenger, the lovely voiced nightingale".[67] As Sappho's fragments yield a profusion of possible interpretations on her life and poetry,

---

[66] Ibid., 23-24.
[67] Fragment Lobel 136.

her fragmentation is exactly the idea behind the nightingale-woman's ability of metamorphosis. This nightingale-woman might actually be the union of Sappho and the nightingale, a shared practice between Swinburne and Shao, which I will discuss in the following section.

1.2.3 A shared practice: the merging of Sappho and the nightingale

In Swinburne's oeuvre the merging of Sappho and the nightingale is most evident in the poem "On the Cliffs", in which the name of Sappho is clearly enunciated:

> [...] inly by thine only name,
> Sappho because I have known thee and loved, hast thou
> None other answer now?
> As brother and sister were we, child and bird,
> Since thy first Lesbian word
> Flamed on me, and I knew not whence I knew
> This was the song that struck my whole soul through,
> Pierced my keen spirit of sense with edge more keen,
> Even when I knew not, even ere sooth was seen,
> When thou wast but the tawny sweet winged thing
> Whose cry was but of spring.[68]

Here "child and bird" denotes that the one being addressed as Sappho might be/was a bird. This is later confirmed by "the tawny sweet winged thing/ Whose cry was but of spring", which could be seen as a rendering of Sappho's fragment Lobel 136 "spring's messenger, the lovely voiced nightingale". It could be interpreted that Sappho is a nightingale, or Sappho used to be a nightingale. However this is interpreted, it is certain that Swinburne likes to merge Sappho with the nightingale. This could be certified by Swinburne's correspondence with Theodore Watts-Dunton,[69] July 30, 1879:

> I have a new poem to read to you [...] I fear there is not overmuch hope of a fresh scandal and consequent "succes de scandale" from a mere rhapsody just four lines short of four hundred (oddly enough) on the song of a nightingale by the sea-side. I don't think I ever told you, did I? my anti-Ovidian theory as to the real personality of that much mis

---

[68] Swinburne, "On the Cliffs", *The Poems of Algernon Charles Swinburne: Volume III* (London: Chatto and Windus, 1904), 318.
[69] Theodore Watts-Dunton was a close friend of Swinburne. In 1879 Swinburne suffered from health problems and was taken care of by Watts-Dunton in Putney.

represented bird - the truth concerning whom dawned upon me one day in my midsummer school holidays, when it flashed on me listening quite suddenly 1) that this was not Philomela - 2) in the same instant, who this was.[70]

The "new poem" here refers to "On the Cliffs". Swinburne claims that the poem is based on an "anti-Ovidian theory" that the nightingale is not Philomela as in Ovid's *Metamorphoses*, nor her sister Procne as in some early Greek sources, but someone whose name he does not enunciate. In his notion, this someone is Sappho. The instance that triggers this theory is his epiphany while listening to a nightingale one day in his college time. The brewing of this theory is documented in the poem "The Nightingale", which I have discussed in the previous section. In the poem, the nightingale is recognized as Sappho only through allusions such as "Leucadia's rock". The name of Sappho is never clearly identified in "The Nightingale" while about twenty years later in "On the Cliffs" there comes "inly by thine own name, Sappho". That is why Swinburne gives an intertextual remark after the enunciation of Sappho' name in "On the Cliffs": "Because I have known thee and loved." This shows that the merging of Sappho and nightingale is a practice that could date back to Swinburne's youth.

The account of "anti-Ovidian theory" bears much resemblance to Shao's story in "Nightingale", which I have talked about in the previous section. Though Shao had personal correspondence with T. J. Wise, the keeper of Swinburne's manuscripts, it is unknown whether he might have heard about the "anti-Ovidian theory" from Wise. There might be a possibility that Shao read Lafourcade's *Swinburne's Hyperion and Other Poems with an Essay on Swinburne and Keats* (1927), which documents this youthful experience of Swinburne. However the influence was transmitted, it is very clear that whenever Shao thinks of the nightingale, he thinks of Sappho concurrently, which is evident in "Nature's Order":

Ah, I wish there were a cruel torture instrument
To cuff her, better with steel shackles,
Chain her hands, feet, eyes and lips,
And lock her in the prison on the Trāyastriṃśa, [71]
So her voice can never reach the human world.
You shouldn't have fed her with ordinary herbs;

---

[70] Lafourcade, *Swinburne's Hyperion and Other Poems with an Essay on Swinburne and Keats*, 148-149.
[71] The thirty-three layers of heaven inhabited by devas, a type of non-human being in Buddhism.

To serve her, have you prepared the food of gods?
Maybe she volunteers to suffer hunger, but
In what name is this hunger? You cannot
Trick her to believe a bamboo cage is a palace in gold;
You can't use a spoon of syrup and make her think
It's grape mash brought from Mytilene.[72]
Because she's just a naive bird that
Doesn't know who loves her would lie to her.

啊，我单愿有残忍的刑具
能加上她，更好是钢铁的枷锁，
枷锁住她的手，脚，眼睛和嘴唇，
把她关闭进三十三天上的牢狱，
叫她的声音永远传不到人间。
本来喂哺她不能用平常的草谷；
侍候她，你可预备着神仙的食粮？
也许她自愿忍受着饥渴，可是
这饥渴有什么名目？你不能用
竹编的笼子骗她是金铸的宫殿；
你不能用一小觚糖水骗她是
打蜜铁铃岛上带来的葡萄浆。
因为她只是一头天真的小鸟，
不知道爱她的会对她说谎。[73]

Here the pronoun "she" denotes a nightingale that has been mentioned in the preceding text. The feeding of herbs and the mentioning of bamboo cage again confirms that this object should be a bird. However, several human body parts are enumerated: hands, feet, lips, which with the female pronoun could be pieced into a female human body. And as Mytilene is identified, this woman is supposed to be Sappho. It is impossible to separate the idea of Sappho from that of a nightingale as the two have been merged in harmony. The nightingale is here rendered concurrently Sappho.

Both Swinburne and Shao regard nature as the perfect paradigm for a condition of harmony in poetry and they both see the nightingale as the ideal symbol for harmony. Harmony is to them the union of meaning and sound, the merging of inner and outer music as Swinburne puts it. The state of harmony

---

[72] Mytilene is the capital of Lesbos. It is often considered as the hometown of Sappho.
[73] Shao, *Poetic Works of Shao Xunmei*, 143-144.

is a condition of music that Shao and Swinburne both aspire to reach with their poetry. Sappho represents the possibility of poetry to Shao and Swinburne. In the youth of the two poets, Sappho served as a muse and a great poet to look up to. As her fragmentation gives room for uncountable possibilities, Sappho is regarded by Shao and Swinburne as the incarnation of poetry and what poetry could be. Both Shao and Swinburne like to merge Sappho and the nightingale in their poetic practices. The merging of Sappho and the nightingale is to them an idea that poetry could reach the condition of harmony, that poetry could be harmonious, like music.

Chapter 2

Shao, Sitwell and "the sister of horticulture"

2.1 Poetry as "the sister of horticulture"

2.1.1 Sitwell's conception of "the sister of horticulture"

The condition of music in poetry is to Shao, or at least to Shao in the 1920s, a state of harmony, the union of meaning and sound, the merging of inner and outer music as Swinburne puts it. But as Sitwell appears on Shao's critical horizon in the 1930s, Shao's idea of the condition of music in poetry gradually evolves into something different. However, it does not mean that the influences of the three writers chosen in this book take place strictly in a chronological order. The three influences are relevant to each other, as their impact on Shao is often combined and synthesized.

Like Swinburne, Sitwell has a similar notion of nature as the perfect paradigm for poetry. She writes: "In reality, the pleasures of poetry are like the joys of nature."[1] The difference between Swinburne's and Sitwell's notions of nature is that the latter puts forth a unique conception of poetry as "the sister of horticulture". Like Swinburne, Sitwell never gives clear definitions of her coined terms. Instead, she uses the phrase in her practices of poetic criticism. Therefore I need to gather and put together the puzzle pieces from her critical corpus in the same way that I handled those of Swinburne. The best way to start this survey is a quote from Sitwell's *Aspects of Modern Poetry:*

> With the Romantics and their more poignant vowel-sense, resulting in a different kind of melodic line, poetry became the sister of music. Now she appears like the sister of horticulture—each poem growing according to the laws of its own nature, but in a line which is more often

---

[1] Edith Sitwell, *The Pleasures of Poetry: A Critical Anthology, Second Series, The Romantic Revival* (New York: W. W. Norton and Company, 1934), 3.

the irregular though entirely natural shape of a tree, —bearing leaves, bearing fruit, —than a sharp melodic line, springing like a fountain.²

Here Sitwell gives a manifesto for poetry as "the sister of horticulture": "each poem growing according to the laws of its own nature." This dictum bears some similarities to Shao's notion that a poem has "her" own life, which is evident in the following excerpt:

> Poetry is not a thesis, not done by research. Her source cannot be verified. We could even say, the writing of poetry is without reason. But we could also say, she has her own research, she has her own verification, she has her own reasons, she has her own world! Her being written, she herself is the owner [...] She has her own life.
>
> 诗不是论文，不是研究来的，她的来是不可考证的。我们更可以说，诗的写出是无理由的。但是，我们也可以说，她有她自己的研究，她有她自己的考证，她有她自己的理由，她有她自己天地！她的写出，她自己是主人[...] 她有她自己的生命。³

As the last sentence indicates, "she", considered by Shao as the personification of poetry, "has her own life". In Sitwell's excerpt, poetry is also personified as a "she" as "she appears like the sister of horticulture". Both Shao and Sitwell deploy the technique of personification and both of them assign the personified poetry a female pronoun. Susan Bordo writes: "Women, besides having bodies, are also associated with the body, which has always been considered woman's 'sphere' in family life, in mythology, in scientific, philosophical, and religious ideology."⁴ Here for Shao and Sitwell, the body is also considered the woman's "sphere" in metapoetics, as both poets associate the body of poetry with women.

However, among the similarities, there lies a nuance. When talking about individual poems in the sentence that comes after the first em dash, namely "each poem growing according to the laws of its own nature", Sitwell uses the pronoun "it" and states that each poem grows according to "its" own nature.

---

² Edith Sitwell, *Aspects of Modern Poetry* (London: Duckworth, 1934), 180.
³ Shao, "Haowen's New Poems" (Haowen de xinshi 浩文的新诗), *Ziyoutan* 自由潭 [The Pool of Freedom] (Shanghai: Shanghai shudian chubanshe, 2012), 269-270. Haowen 浩文 is a pseudonym of Shao. This article is interesting as it is written by Shao and comments on the poems published under his own pseudonym.
⁴ Susan Bordo, *Unbearable Weight: Feminism, Western Culture, and the Body* (Berkeley: University of California Press, 1993), 143.

Here Sitwell is comparing individual poems to plants, as plants are rarely gendered when they are addressed. Though her conception of "the sister of horticulture" involves both "sister" and "horticulture", her focus is for sure the latter. In contrast, Shao's understanding seems to glide towards the word "sister", as in the excerpt, he does not give any explicit allusions to horticulture, yet. Later in this chapter, I will analyze some poems of Shao which manifest a clear association with the notion of horticulture, though, Sitwell's conception in Shao's reception eventually morphs into a strange yet unique practice of "the horticulture of sisters".[5]

It should also be noted that while Swinburne's nature refers to the wild entirety of nature, Sitwell's notion of horticulture denotes the existence of a garden. The garden is considered by Sitwell as a micro-nature. Though the plant in a garden grows "according to the laws of its own nature", just like plants growing in wild nature, a garden is in need of a gardener and it is supposed to yield, "bearing leaves, bearing fruit", while the unmanaged wild nature does not promise any return. McGann makes an interesting observation: "The natural world for Swinburne is [...] a vast and complex autopoetic machine whose 'growth ha[s] no guerdon/ But only to grow' ("Hertha," ll. 138-139)."[6] Swinburne's notion of nature as the perfect paradigm of harmony is only a criterion in poetry criticism. It does not yield a methodology on how this condition of harmony could be achieved. In comparison, Sitwell's garden involves the effort of a gardener and aims for a guerdon.

Interestingly, Swinburne makes his point on nature with examples of Romantic poets such as Blake, Shelley and Wordsworth, while Sitwell also brings in a discussion of Romantic poets to illustrate her proposal of "the sister of horticulture". As one sees in the excerpt from *Aspects of Modern Poetry*, Romantic poetry is considered by her to be "the sister of music". However, "the sister of horticulture" does not mean an exclusion of music, but rather a modification of music. "The sister of music" is not entirely a compliment as Sitwell dislikes the uncontrolled, spontaneous springing of sharp melodic lines, which in her opinion, is characteristic of Romantic poetry. A case of exception would be that of Shelley, whom she discusses in *The Romantic Revival*:

> In Shelley's lyrics, for instance, the actual variations in the texture resemble, not so much the differences between silk and marble and stone, as the differences between the perfume of lily, dark rose, tuberose, violet and narcissus. These melodic effects are the result, in part, of his vowel-schemes, built up, often, on a foundation of two vowels only, or

---

[5] "The horticulture of sisters" is my term rather than Shao's.
[6] McGann, "Wagner, Baudelaire, Swinburne: Poetry in the Condition of Music", 631.

on a foundation of two vowels in which each vowel is used both poignantly and dulled. But the beauty of the poems is often as intangible as the scent of the flowers, and is not to be explained.[7]

Here she puts forth a conception of "texture" without any attempt to define it. She observes that the "melodic effects" of Shelley's poetry are only "in part" the result of his vowel-schemes. The other part that contributes to the music of Shelley's poetry is considered by her as something "not to be explained". The inexplicability of this part is compared by her with the intangibility of the scent of flowers. Note the appearance of garden flowers. The texture of Shelley's poems, in her opinion, resembles the perfume of a group of garden flowers: lily, dark rose, tuberose, violet and narcissus. One could deduce that texture is termed by Sitwell as something that is only related to sound "in part", and it does not simply concern the meaning of a poem, either. It is something that transcends the dichotomy of meaning and sound, or that of inner and outer music as Swinburne puts it.

In Shao's works he does not have a systematic judgement of Romantic poetry, for the majority of poetry that he reads is late Victorian and early Modernist poetry. It can be deduced that his knowledge and reception of Romantic poetry, including Shelley, is influenced by the judgements made by Victorians and the early modernists. It is an interesting coincidence that Swinburne's notion of inner and outer music is also put forth in a piece of criticism on Shelley ("his depths and heights of inner and outer music are as divine as nature's"),[8] which I have discussed in the first chapter. It is unknown whether Sitwell had read Swinburne's words before she wrote hers. But if one reads the two excerpts against each other, Sitwell's notion of texture could be seen as a state of interweave in the merging of inner and outer music, the union of meaning and sound. Texture is neither inner nor outer; it traverses between the two.

2.1.2 Texture and *jili* 肌理

In a survey of the reception of the idea of texture in Republican China, Chen Yue 陈越 points out that Shao was among the earliest critics in China to write about this term.[9] The earliest account by Shao is an essay entitled "New Poetry and 'Texture'" (Xinshi yu jili 新诗与"肌理") published in *Human Words Weekly*

---

[7] Sitwell, *The Romantic Revival*, 11-12.
[8] Swinburne, *Essays and Studies* (London: Chatto and Windus, 1875), 215.
[9] Chen Yue 陈越, "Zhongguo xiandai shixuezhong de jilishuo" 中国现代诗学中的肌理说 [Texture in Modern Chinese Poetics], in *Zhongguo xiandai wenxue yanjiu congkan* 中国现代文学研究丛刊 [Modern Chinese Literature Studies] issue 3 (2014): 107-121.

(Renyan zhoukan 人言周刊) in December 1935. He writes: "Sitwell emphasizes the texture of poetry [...] She published three series of *The Pleasures of Poetry* [...] In these three series she wields the term frequently." ("西脱惠尔最注重二诗的 texture [...] 西脱惠尔曾辑《诗的愉快》三部 [...] 她在这三部选集里，便尽量发挥她对于"肌理"之主张。")[10] From this account, one could confirm that Shao had read the three series of *The Pleasures of Poetry*, namely *Milton and the Augustan Age*, *The Romantic Revival* and *The Victorian Age*. Considering that *The Pleasures of Poetry* was released in 1934, Shao's essay was of useful immediacy. He writes subsequently in the essay: "A true poet should know not just the literal meanings of a word, but more importantly how to physically feel and comprehend the sound, the color, the scent and the temperature of a word." ("一个真正的诗人非特对于字的意义应当明白，更重要的是对于一个字的声音、颜色、嗅昧、温度，都要能肉体地去感觉及领悟。")[11] As Shao maintains that a poet should be able to feel the "scent" of a word, this statement resonates with Sitwell's use of the term texture to compare Shelley's poetry with the scent of flowers. In *The Romantic Revival* she writes that "the beauty of the poems is often as intangible as the scent of the flowers", which I have discussed in the previous section. An occasion where Shao puts the term texture into a similar practice is his comment on the poems of Stephen Spender[12] in the column "Words on Arts" (Yiwen xianhua 艺文闲话) in *Human Words Weekly*. He writes that his poetry "is like cyan grass after a rain, whose voluble color carries a twinkling shine. It's like a new-shot bamboo on a barren hill; the husk is tender, but you know the texture's hard." ("像是雨后的青草，流利的颜色里带着闪耀的光芒；像是荒山里的新竹，衣壳是柔嫩的，但是你明白他质地的坚硬。")[13] Here Shao compares Spender's poetry to "cyan grass after a rain", which is again a plant, and uses the color and the touch of the grass and bamboo to denote the quality of Spender's poetry. This shows that Shao understands the term the same way Sitwell does and puts it into critical practice in a similar way.

Shao's understanding of texture might also be influenced by some other sources concurrently. If one returns to "New Poetry and 'Texture'", one could see that Shao uses the word *jili* 肌理 as the Chinese translation of Sitwell's texture, the practice of which as he admits was first done by Qian Zhongshu 钱钟书: "Sitwell most emphasizes the texture of poetry (the word texture was once

---

[10] Shao, *Collected Works of Shao Xunmei*, 134.
[11] Ibid., 134-135.
[12] Stephen Harold Spender (1909-1995) was a British poet and literary critic. His famous works include the poetry collections *Poems* (1933) and *The Still Centre* (1939).
[13] Originally published in *Human Words Weekly* 2, no. 15 (1935); here quoted from *Conversations of One Man*, 93.

translated as jili by Qian Zhongshu)" ("西脱惠尔最注重于诗的 Texture {这 Texture 一字，曾由钱钟书先生译为肌理}").[14] However, the word *jili* is not Qian's coinage. In "Imperfect Understanding" (Bugou zhiji 不够知己), a review article of Wen Yuanning's 温源宁[15] *Imperfect Understanding* published in June 1935 (that is, six months before Shao published "New Poetry and 'Texture'"), Qian compares the writing styles of Wen and William Hazlitt.[16] He remarks: "Mr. Wen's 'jili' (Weng Tanxi[17]'s critical term concerning poetry; there is no ready word better than this to translate Edith Sitwell's texture) seems to be not as thick as Hazlitt's." ("温先生的 '肌理' {翁覃谿论诗的名词，把它来译 Edith Sitwell 所谓 texture, 没有更好的成语了}似乎也不如夏士烈德来的稠密。")[18] Qian states in the parenthesis the word *jili*, which could be literally translated as "flesh grain", is a loan from Weng Fanggang 翁方纲.[19] Weng's proposal of this term was at first an attempt to defy the 18th-century literati's obsession with two dominant schools of literary criticism that focus on the "spirit" (Shenyun 神韵) and "tone" (Gediao 格调) of poetry, advocated respectively by Wang Shizhen 王士禛[20] and Shen Deqian 沈德潜[21]. Han Sheng 韩胜 observes that Weng's *jili* was first used

---

[14] Shao, *Collected Works of Shao Xunmei*, 134.

[15] Wen Yuanning (1899-1984) was a lesser-known author and literary critic. He was educated in Cambridge and became Qian's teacher when he taught in Tsinghua University.

[16] William Hazlitt (1778-1830) was a British literary critic. His most critically-aclaimed works include the monograph *Characters of Shakespear's Plays* (1817) and a collection of essays entitled *Table-Talk* (1821).

[17] Tanxi 覃谿 is the art name of Weng Fanggang 翁方纲.

[18] Qian Zhongshu 钱钟书, Xiezai rensheng bianshang rensheng bianshang de bianshang shiyu 写在人生边上 人生边上的边上 石语 [On the Edge of Life, The Edge of the Edge of Life, Stone Talks] (Beijing: Sanlian shudian, 2002), 336.

[19] Weng Fanggang (1733-1818) was an author, epigraphist and literary critic in Qing Dynasty. He was famous for his conception of Jili 肌理 in poetry criticism and also for his achievements in textology, epigraphy and calligraphy.

[20] Wang Shizhen (1634-1711) was an author and statesman in early Qing Dynasty. He was notable for establishing a school of poetry criticism that pivots on his conception of "spirit" (Shenyun 神韵). He never gives any clear definition for the term Shenyun. His conception of Shenyun could be best summarized as something that denotes a condition of a piece of work that could only be perceived intuitively, instead of analytically.

[21] Shen Deqian (1673-1769) was an author and statesman in Qing Dynasty. He emphasizes the importance of poetry's acoustic features and maintains that a poem's "tone" (Gediao 格调), a personified quality that governs the poem's holistic vocality, will benefit from the clever deployment of the poem's acoustic features. He states that Tang poetry, with its majestic eloquence and its variety, should be the perfect model for poetry practitioners.

as a metaphor in contrast to bones and flesh until he developed it into a theory of writing poetry that focuses on the careful screening of words and the organic assembly of words to form a holistic whole that benefits from the well-calculated interweaving of words; the quality of such interconnection is *jili*.[22] In this sense, *jili* has the same implication as Sitwell's conception of texture when they are both applied to poetry. The difference would be that *jili* gives a clear allusion to human physiology which Sitwell's texture does not.

Besides Qian, Shi Zhecun 施蛰存[23] is also a contemporary of Shao who uses the word *jili* in literary criticism.[24] In 1933 Shi published an article that comments on the poems in the journal *Les Contemporains* (Xiandai 现代): 'The poems in *Les Contemporains* are mostly unrhymed and with irregular lines, but they all have very perfect 'jili' (texture). They are modern poems. They are poems!" ("《现代》中的诗,大多是没有韵的,句子也很不整齐,但它们都有相当完美的"肌理" (Texture), 它们是现代的诗, 是诗!")[25] Though Shi does place the word "texture" in brackets beside *jili*, he does not mention Sitwell anywhere in the article, and hence it is uncertain whether this instance of texture accords with the one conceptualized by Sitwell. Chen points out that Robert Graves[26] also talks about a notion of texture, along with diction, meter, rhyme and structure in *Contemporary Techniques of Poetry: A Political Analogy* (1925),[27] in which he defines texture as the relationship between vowels and consonants in sounds.[28]

---

[22] Han Sheng 韩胜, "Weng Fanggang de shige xuanping yu 'jili'shuo de xingcheng" 翁方纲的诗歌选评与"肌理"说的形成 [On a Selection of Weng Fanggang's Poetry and the Formation of 'Jili'"], in *Zhongguo wenxue yanjiu* 中国文学研究 [Chinese Literature Studies] volume 3 (2009), 65.

[23] Shi Zhecun (1905-2003) was a writer, art critic and one of the most important figures among the New Sensationists (Xinganjue pai 新感觉派), a group of modernist writers active in the late 20s and the 30s. Other members of the group include Liu Na'ou 刘呐鸥 and Mu Shiying 穆时英. Shi was educated in Shanghai University and Zhendan University. In his works he often employs psychoanalysis, the techniques of montage and stream of consciousness. His most critically-acclaimed works include the collections of short stories *The General's Head* (Jiangjun di tou 将军底头) (1932) and *An Evening of Spring Rain* (Meiyu zhi xi 梅雨之夕) (1933).

[24] Chen, "Texture in Modern Chinese Poetics", 112.

[25] Shi Zhecun 施蛰存, "Youguanyu benkanzhong de shi" 又关于本刊中的诗 [About the Poems in the Journal], in Xiandai 现代 [Les Contemporains] 4, no. 1 (1933): 6-7.

[26] Robert Graves (1895-1985) was a British writer. His famous works include the biography *Lawrence and the Arabs* (1927) and a novel entitled *I, Claudius* (1934).

[27] Robert Graves, *Contemporary Techniques of Poetry: A Political Analogy* (London: Hogarth, 1925).

[28] Chen, "Texture in Modern Chinese Poetics", 108.

As Shi in the article talks about rhyme and regularity of lines, as evident in phrases such as "mostly unrhymed" and "with irregular lines", it is likely that Shi understands texture as something that could be juxtaposed with the discussion of "rhyme" and "regularity". This understanding of texture is similar to Graves' and different from Sitwell's.

Other than "New Poetry and 'Texture'", Shao published an article "On Texture" (Lun jili 论肌理) in "Friday on Poetry" (Jinyao shihua 金曜诗话),[29] a column he wrote from 1938 to 1939 in *China-US Daily* (Zhongmei ribao 中美日报).[30] It could be deduced from that article that Shao's understanding of texture is informed by Sitwell, Qian and Graves.

Qian holds that a unique characteristic of Chinese conventional literary criticism, which would include the theory of Weng, is the humanization or animization of literature. He supplies his argument with many excerpts from ancient texts that talk about literature in the discourse of human body, and states that "we think of literature as living being of our kind" ("我们把文章看成我们自己同类的活人").[31] He writes further:

> The appreciation of all arts is at its core Einfühlung [...] The humanization of literary criticism is just the product when Einfühlung has reached its vertex. Indeed there are no concepts of science, literature, philosophy, outlooks on life and the universe that do not originate from Einfühlung. Our comprehension of the world is but metaphoric, symbolic, als ob and poetic. To put it in a simple metaphor, it's like a child who wants to see the light in the mirror while he finds himself in the light. The human from the beginning has soaked himself into the world, drilled himself into things, built up categories and concepts. Some of the concepts have gradually become hard and framed, lost their humanity, like a fish fossilized. Till natural sciences are developed, thinkers turn the epistemology of our predecessors the other way around, chain hearts with things and use the scientific concept of fish fossils to suppress the water of fishpond [...] Einfühlung and pan-objectivism, behaviorism and idealism, are just the up and down of one wave, the variations of one principle.

---

[29] Nine pieces of Jinyao shihua was republished as "Jinyao shihua jiuze" 金曜诗话(九则) [Nine Pieces of Friday on Poetry] in *Shi tansuo* 诗探索 [Poetry Exploration] no. 1 (2010): 23-36.

[30] The article was divided in three parts and published on 20 Jan, 27 Jan, 3 Feb, 1939.

[31] Qian, *On the Edge of Life, the Edge of the Edge of Life, Stone Talks*, 119.

> 一切艺术鉴赏根本就是移情作用 (Einfühlung) [...] 人化文评不过是移情作用发达到最高点的产物。其实一切科学、文学、哲学、人生观、宇宙观的概念，无不根源着移情作用。我们对于世界的认识，不过是一种比喻、象征的、像煞有介事的 (als ob)、诗意的认识。用一个粗浅的比喻，好像小孩子要看镜子的光明，却在光明里发现了自己。人类最初把自己沁透了世界，把心钻进了物，建设了范畴概念；这许多概念慢慢地变硬变定，失掉本来的人性，仿佛鱼化了石。到自然科学发达，思想家把初民的认识方法翻了过来，把物来统制心，把鱼化石的科学概念来压塞养鱼的活水 [...] 移情作用跟泛客观 (pan-objectivism)；行为主义跟唯心论，只是一个波浪的起伏，一个原则的变化。[32]

Regarding the "the humanization of literary criticism", Shao puts forth a similar statement: "We must first admit the physiological conditions of a word. It has historical background. It is material. It has shapes and colors. Its sound could be soft or hard. It has weight. It has temperature." ("须先承认一个'字'的生理上的条件;它是有历史背景的; 它是物质的; 它是有形状颜色，声音软硬，轻重和冷热的 。")[33] These "physiological conditions" provide a foundation for the discussion of a poem's texture.

Shao affirms Sitwell's proposal that a poet needs to work the texture of a poem, but he refuses the over-emphasis on texture as a poet cannot mistake "the means to write poetry as the end of poetry" ("把写诗的手段，误作写诗的目的").[34] He states that the notion of texture is "meant to let poetry gain life" ("这种技巧本来是使诗得到生命的"), but the abuse of it would "sentence poetry to death so it would be just an empty coffin" ("反而为诗宣告了死刑，从此的诗便只剩下了空虚的棺椁").[35]

Shao was influenced by Sitwell when it comes to the notion of texture, though his understanding of texture is merged with Weng's idea of *jili* refreshed by Qian. Sitwell proposes that poetry as "the sister of horticulture" should grow naturally, an idea that is inspired by the life cycle of a plant. Shao adds a twist of human physiology into this plant, which morphs into the kind of amorous poems that I will examine in the next section.

---

[32] Ibid., 131.
[33] Chen, "Texture in Modern Chinese Poetics", 115.
[34] Ibid., 118.
[35] Ibid., 118.

2.2 The horticulture of musical sisters

2.2.1 The flower as musical woman

Just as Swinburne prefers the symbol of the bird, Sitwell also has her signature symbol, which is cast in a poem entitled "Metamorphosis":

> And dark as Asia, now, is Beauty's daughter,
> The rose, once clear as music o'er deep water.
> Now the full moon her fire and light doth spill
> On turkey-plumaged leaves and window-sill,
> On leaves that seem the necks and plumes of urban
> Turkeys, each a Sultan in a turban,
> And strawberries among the beavers' wool[36]

Note the presence of the rose as a flower symbol. The rose here does not refer to merely the flower bud of a rose, but the entirety of the plant. The rose was once "clear as music": the rose and music are rendered in an equation with the aid of an adjective "clear". The adjective "clear" has multiple meanings, and the meanings are different when it is coupled with the rose and music respectively. The word "clear" weaves together the rose and music, two entities which one would not usually consider as a set of metaphor. This act of interweaving forms the texture of "the rose is clear as music", which is significantly different from the mere accumulation of "the rose is clear" and "the music is clear". In this unexpected set of metaphor, the rose shares the quality of "clear" with music through their joint texture. Note that the rose here is also "beauty's daughter", and therefore personified and gendered. The personified rose here is regarded by Sitwell as the incarnation of music. This incarnation of music is then capable of metamorphosing into other things, such as a turkey. This metamorphosis is aided again by texture: a turkey's plumage resembles the leaves of a rose under moonlight. The resemblance lies in not just the colour or shape of the plumage and leaves, but a union of these qualities which people tend to think as separate. The union of these qualities weaves the turkey plumage and the rose leaves in a gathering whose significance lies in their joint texture. Likewise, this turkey is further metamorphosed into "a Sultan in a turban", not by a clear enunciation of any similarity in the separate qualities of contour or posture, but through their shared texture. Through the shared texture, the various forms of the metamorphosis are interwoven within the texture of the poem. The apprehension of the texture would be an epiphany of the poem's significance,

---

[36] Sitwell, *The Collected Poems of Edith Sitwell* (London: Duckworth, 1931), 78.

the fruit that the rose yields. As the rose is the incarnation of music, what the rose yields is a significance that resembles the condition of music.

Similarly, the flower is also considered by Shao as an incarnation of music. He writes in a poem entitled "Flower" (Hua 花):

> It's full of poetry's beauty,
> The concrete of soundless music;
> Even with no other contribution made,
> It has done life's duty.

> 他充满了诗词的美丽，
> 是无声的音乐的具体；
> 便没别的贡献添助，
> 也尽了生命的义务。[37]

As Shao regards the flower as "the concrete", the specific form of the abstract "soundless music", he denotes that the flower is an incarnation of music. The juxtaposition of "full of poetry's beauty", "the concrete of soundless music" and "done life's duty" establishes a trinity of poetry, music and life. The three entities are interconnected through their joint texture. Poetry should be flowery, and therefore musically beautiful, which resonates with Sitwell's rendering of the rose in "Metamorphosis". "Life's duty" can be deemed as Shao's response to Sitwell's notion that poetry growing naturally should be "bearing leaves, bearing fruit". It can be interpreted as the reproduction of life, as flower is the reproductive organ of a plant. However, in Shao's poetry, the reproductive function of the flower usually has a sexual denotation.

Plants are substantially cultivated in Shao's works and tightly entangled with the idea of a woman's body, which suggests a synthesis of various influences. Notably, in *Roses and Roses* Shao translates "A Match" from Swinburne, and I have talked about an excerpt regarding the match of bird and song in the first chapter. This poem has another stanza that features the thriving of roses and leaves:

> If love were what the rose is,
> And I were like the leaf,
> Our lives would grow together
> In sad or singing weather,
> Blown fields or flowerful closes,

---

[37] Ibid., 23.

Green pasture or gray grief;
If love were what the rose is,
And I were like the leaf.

要是爱是玫瑰花，
而我和叶子一般，
我们的生命当相相长在
忧郁或是歌唱的气候里，
含苞的园或是开花的场里，
绿的快活或是灰的愁苦里，
要是爱是玫瑰花，
而我和叶子一般。[38]

The collage of colors and abstract ideas evident in "gray grief" is a characteristic of Swinburne, and the presence of "singing weather" links the synesthetic texture of the plants to music. Just as the title of the collection *Roses and Roses* suggests, the featured poetry translations are all deemed by Shao as roses. In "A Match" roses and songs are mutually inclusive. "Love" and "I" live in a symbiosis similar to the cohabitation of roses and leaves, which is reminiscent of Sitwell's "Metamorphosis". Likewise, this conception of love as symbiosis is frequently played with in Shao's garden poems, such as "Tomorrow" (Mingtian 明天):

White dews all kiss the grass,
The grass giggles;
Kissing and hugging,
Hugging till a muddle.

白露儿尽吻着青草，
青草格格笑；
吻着又拥抱，
拥抱到相相混沌了。[39]

Dew and grass are here rendered in love. The relationship is organic as they are organized by a symbiotic connection that is mutually beneficial. This is the

---

[38] Shao, *Roses and Roses*, 22.
[39] Shao, *Poetic Works of Shao Xunmei*, 105.

thriving side of organicity. Notably, Shao also translates in *Roses and Roses* Sara Teasdale's "November", which seems gloomy and mirthless:

> The world is tired, the year is old,
> The little leaves are glad to die,
> The wind goes shivering with cold
> Among the rushes dry.

> 世界倦了年岁老了，
> 将死的叶情愿死了，
> 凛凛的风翩翩飘过
> 那已经枯了的芦梢。

> Our love is dying like the grass,
> And we who kissed grow coldly kind,
> Half glad to see our poor love pass
> Like leaves along the wind.

> 我们的爱草般萎了，
> 曾吻过的我们冷了，
> 欣欣看着旧情逝去
> 像落叶被风儿卷跑。 40

The drying of rushes, the falling of leaves and the withering of grass all denote the decomposition of life. The loss of life is compared to the loss of love, which could be seen as an antiphony to Swinburne's well-planted love. This declining side of organicity also occurs in many of Shao's poems, which I will talk about later. Besides, the collection features three translations of Verlaine, "Spleen", "Green" and "Colloque sentimental", the former two of which both have something to do with the horticulture of love:

> Spleen
>
> Les roses étaient toutes rouges
> Et les lierres étaient tout noirs.
> Chère, pour peu que tu te bouges,
> Renaissent tous mes désespoirs.

---

40 Shao, *Roses and Roses*, 26.

玫瑰花这般的绯红,
百合的颜色吓深深。
爱吓你的恐惧将缠得
我底死了的烦恼重生。

[...]

Du houx à la feuille vernie
Et du luisant buis je suis las,
Et de la campagne infinie
Et de tout, fors de vous, hélas!

冬青的树我已不爱,
长绿的草我已厌恶,
一切的景致我均生憎,
只有你吓是我底心肉!⁴¹

Green

Voici des fruits, des fleurs, des feuilles et des branches
Et puis voici mon coeur qui ne bat que pour vous.
Ne le déchirez pas avec vos deux mains blanches
Et qu'à vos yeux si beaux l'humble présent soit doux.

看吓这些果儿花儿叶儿枝儿,
看吓我底心只为了你而跳动,
啊请勿以你底白手撕碎了它,
让它也变成甜蜜在你底眼中。⁴²

In "Spleen" the roses and ivy are tangled with love and sorrow; so are holly and boxwood with weariness. Specific plants and abstract ideas are tangled up. In "Green" an imperative is given, which involves bodily contacts with the plant. This plant-human interaction also recurs in Shao's poetry, which this book will deal with later. In comparison with the poems listed above, the difference of Shao's garden lies in the treatment that it is often coupled with a presence of

---

[41] Ibid., 9.
[42] Ibid., 10.

dream. He writes in "Green Escaped the Plantain" (Lü taoqule bajiao 绿逃去了芭蕉):

> Green escaped the plantain, red escaped the rose,
> No more can I find drunkenness in colors;
> Maybe there'll be a day or night,
> She'll take me back to yesterday's dream's reign.

> 绿逃去了芭蕉，红逃去了蔷薇，
> 我再不能在色彩中找到醉迷；
> 也许会有一个白日或是黑夜，
> 她将我领回昨天的梦的国里。[43]

Here the poetic voice aspires to enter a state of dream where the colors of the plantain and the rose are more intoxicating and thus, he could "find drunkenness in colours". The poetic voice here is moaning over the loss of the state of dream, while in a poem entitled "Xunmei's Dream" (Xunmei de meng 洵美的梦) the voice is eagerly wishing for the coming-true of the dream. In the latter poem, the poetic voice enters a dream (in the sense of a state of dream):

> This is my hope, my wish: now, she
> Really comes; she brings me gently into
> A forest, I've been here, it's
> The edge of heaven, near the center of hell.
>
> I see again the twigs that I kissed,
> The grass and shrubs on which I sat.
> I've also bathed once in that spring,
> The valley still holds my first sung song.

> 这是我的希望，我的想：现在，她
> 真的来了；她带了我轻轻走进
> 一座森林，我是来过的，这已是
> 天堂的边沿，将近地狱的中心。
>
> 我又见到我曾经吻过的树枝，
> 曾经坐过的草和躺过的花阴，

---

[43] Shao, *Poetic Works of Shao Xunmei*, 163.

我也曾经在那泉水里洗过澡，
山谷还抱着我第一次的歌声。[44]

She the dream comes, literally: a dream (wish) is asked for and a dream (state) is granted. The text unfolds as the dream (state) of the poetic voice, when simultaneously "I" enter a realm as the unfolding text. The dream (wish) only comes true in the dream (state); the dream (state) fulfills what "I" have dreamed/wished: a forest permeated with music is given. The music here is represented by "my first sung song". Have "I" already been here? Why is here a song that "I" already sang? Note the use of tense in the excerpt. There seems to be a sense of confusion here: the poetic voice claims that "I" have been here, which could never be as she the dream comes to "me" for the very first time. But this dream (state) does look like the dream (wish) that "I" have dreamed/wished earlier. This is not a confusion of time or causality. It comes from the tangling of two bodies, one being the textual body constituted by the dream (state) and the other being "I", a body that is presumably human. "I" am bodily connected to the plants, the constituents of the dream (state), through the act of touching (kissing, sitting on). Hence the body of "I" is tangled with the textual body. One might wonder why "I" would like to kiss twigs. The dream (state) is the outcome of the coming of she the dream and an embodiment of her. The twigs to the dream (state) could hence be seen the hair to a woman, that is, she the dream. In this sense, kissing twigs is a textual play that is at the same time highly sexual. This kind of intimacy with plants occurs and recurs in many of Shao's poems.

Unlike the fact that nightingale is cast as the ideal bird symbol, Shao does not have an obsession with any particular species of plants. In Shao's oeuvre, there is a variety of poems that are named after various species of flowers. He works the texture of these poems to make each poem significant in their respective union with the title flower. The most impressive one among them would have to be "Peony" (Mudan 牡丹):

Peony could die
But her virgin-like red,
Her slut-like swing,
Enough to craze you and me in daytime,
And dream in dark night.

What is lacking is scent:
Though she did add some sweetness in poems,

---

[44] Ibid., 132.

Mix some cheating in tears,
But I can never forget the damp flesh,
The rosy skin,
The tight-squeezed drunkenness.

牡丹也是会死的
但是她那童贞般的红，
淫妇般的摇动，
尽够你我白日里去发疯，
黑夜里去做梦。

少的是香气:
虽然她亦曾在诗句里加进些甜味，
在眼泪里和入些诈欺，
但是我总忘不了那潮润的肉，
那透红的皮，
那紧挤出来的醉意。[45]

To Shao the texture of a peony lies in the blending of its color of red and the motion of swinging in the wind. What should be noted is that the adoption of the pronoun "she" and the terms "virgin-like red" and "the rosy skin" allude to the body of a woman, as the color of the peony is compared to the skin tone of a woman. Phrases like "slut-like swing", "craze in daytime" and "dream in dark night" link the swinging motion of the flower to an erotic fantasy of a woman engaged in sexual acts. In this way a peony and a woman are merged by their shared texture.

Besides, there is another layer in the signification of swinging. Being a poem "Peony" swings line to line as the length of each line keeps changing in a manner that resembles the motion of waving. The juxtaposition of the dichotomies "you and I", "slut and virgin" and "daytime and dark night" strengthens the sense of swinging back and forth. Therefore the peony, the woman and the poem are united in a significant trinity through their shared texture. This trinity is, as "slut and virgin" suggests, concurrently penetrable and impenetrable; it is highly playful and rejects a univocal interpretation. Notably, the peony-woman also appears in a poem entitled "Hair" (Toufa 头发):

---

[45] Shao, *Poetic Works of Shao Xunmei*, 153.

On cheeks white as a snow mountain arctic,
Drifts a soft wave of light red peonies;
Eyes, brows' tip and chignon,
Like an otter resting on the bank.

[…]

Ah lovers' hair,
Knot in lovers' mind;
Ah lovers in this shortest fastest time,
Seconds and minutes just to solve this endless knot.

啊这北极雪山般白的颊上，
漂来一层淡红芍药色的轻浪；
那眼球眉梢及发髻，
又像水獭休息在岸旁。

[…]

啊情人的头发吓，
在情人心中打着结；
情人在这最短最快的时光里吓，
分分秒秒只是去解这无穷的结吧。[46]

Here "a soft wave of light red peonies" denotes the same texture that I have talked about: the blending of the color of red and the motion of swinging. And when this sentence of "a soft wave of light red peonies" is interwoven with "cheeks" into the texture of the poem, it denotes a blush on the face of a woman. There are two more matches in the excerpt: white cheeks and a snow mountain, chignon and an otter that rests ashore. Multiple matches of symbols are interwoven, like hair, in the texture of this poem named "Hair" and form a knot. This knot could not be unwound. To unwind the knot is to unwind the interwoven texture of the poem, which will only lead to the decomposition of writing.

The texture of a poem could not be torn apart without harming its significance. This idea is made more clear in "Narcissus" (Shuixian he 水仙吓),

---

[46] Ibid., 80.

Shao, Sitwell and "the sister of horticulture"

in which a flower-woman, instead of a man to whom narcissus usually alludes, is grounded by the texture of mud:

> Narcissus!
> Since you were born in this dirty mud,
> Why do you have this scent,
> That makes me passing by want to love you?
>
> Narcissus!
> I step in the mud to kiss you,
> But how can I pick you up?
> You've fallen in this dirty mud!
>
> 水仙吓!
> 你既然生在这污浊的泥里,
> 为什么还要有这一些的香气,
> 竟使过路的我也想爱你?
>
> 水仙吓!
> 我踏进了泥里把嘴来吻你,
> 但我又怎能将你采起?
> 你早已落在这污浊的泥里![47]

Here a flower-woman is merged with the texture of dirty mud. Each stanza starts with a call-out of "Narcissus", the name of the flower-woman. Yet her rhizome is deeply rooted in the mud of three long, heavy sentences. She cannot come to "me". The rhizome is trapped in the mud of language, which elicits a self-referential remark from the poetic voice: "You've fallen in this dirty mud!" Narcissus is unable to be picked up as her significance, the trinity of her life, poem and music lies in the act of rooting in the mud of language. Therefore an act of picking would simply lead to a laceration of the poem's texture, a fatal incision of the flesh from the bones and hence the decomposition of language.

And note the title "Narcissus" and its cultural underpinning. Bordo cites from art historian John Berger that in various Western artistic representations such as literature and painting, usually "men act and women appear." She writes:

> Women exist to be seen, and they know it—a notion communicated by the constant tropes of female narcissism: women shown preening,

---

[47] Ibid., 82.

looking in mirrors, stroking their own bodies, exhibiting themselves for an assumed spectator. "Do I look good? Do you like me? Am I pretty?" the women in the pictures seem to be saying. Women are supposed to care about such things, these images tell us.[48]

In "Narcissus" the male poetic voice asks the narcissus-woman "Why do you have this scent, / That makes me passing by want to love you", as if the flower-woman deliberately seduces the male "I" by putting on some fragrance, preening and exhibiting herself. And as the narcissus cannot move but the male "I" can "pass by", "step in the mud" and pick up flowers, her immobility and his agency forms a contrast that is similar to Berger's "men act and women appear" pattern. This pattern and the imagined female narcissism, however, is the manifestation of male narcissism. Drawing in the works of de Beauvoir, Bordo writes:

> De Beauvoir argued that within the social world, there are those who occupy the unmarked position of the "essential," the universal, the human, and those who are defined, reduced and marked by their (sexual, racial, religious) differences from that norm. The accomplishments of those who are so marked - of the Other - may not always be disdained; often, they will be appreciated, but always in their special and peripheral place, the place of their difference.[49]

"Those who occupy the unmarked position of the 'essential', the universal, the human" are men. The narcissus-woman in the poem is grounded in the mud, "reduced and marked" by her sexual differences from the norm of the male voice, and only appreciated by the male "I" in the mud, the "special and peripheral place" of her difference. The narcissus-woman here is no exhibitionist, but being exhibited.

Based on these poems, one can deduce that Shao understands clearly Sitwell's notion of texture and the way she uses the flower as a symbol. However, in Shao's practices, there evolves something different from Sitwell's rendering of flower, or I can say his reception of Sitwell's influence somehow goes awry, as seen in the instances of peony and narcissus—an equation of flower with sexual consummation.

---

[48] Susan Bordo, "Gay Men's Revenge", *The Journal of Aesthetics and Art Criticism* 1999, vol. 57, no. 1: 21.
[49] Susan Bordo, "The Feminist as Other", *Metaphilosophy* 1996, vol. 27, no. 1-2: 12.

2.2.2 Sexual consummation as a condition of music

Though Sitwell often personifies her flowers as women, she does not use any word that alludes to sexual activities. In comparison, Shao's flower-women are often situated in an erotic setting. With the use of texture, Shao s(t)imulates sexual acts through the interaction of the poetic voice and the flower-woman and yields an effect of sexual consummation, which is to him a synonym for the condition where poetry is musical. This could be seen in a poem entitled "Spring" (Chun 春):

> Now the flower's scent brings a fleshy air,
> Silent rain threads ooze a hint of lust;
> In the bath I hate to see my sinful skin,
> Ah how can the body's crimson be wiped off?

> 啊这时的花香总带着肉气,
> 不说话的雨丝也含着淫意;
> 沐浴恨见自己的罪的肌肤,
> 啊身上的绯红怎能擦掉去?[50]

Here the marriage of "flower's scent" with "fleshy air" gives the former a sense of aphrodisiac. And the rain threads that "ooze a hint of lust" seem to allude to body fluid outflown in sexual acts. "The body's crimson" is again ambiguous: it could be blood from a human body (in this mise-en-scene presumably the blood caused by sexual intercourse) or simply a color left by the flowers used in the bath. This ambiguity is one of Shao's characteristic tricks, and it is done with an emphasis on the shared texture of blood and flowers used in the bath. Now let us look back at the lines in "Flower", a poem which I have discussed earlier: "It's [The flower] full of poetry's beauty,/ The concrete of soundless music". As Shao regards the flower as an incarnation of music, having sex with the flower-woman seems to him a way that leads to reproduction, that is, the reproduction of a condition of music in poetry. He equates the sexual consummation between the poetic voice and the flower-woman with the acquisition of the condition of music in poetry, which can be exemplified by "The Poem of Love" (Qingshi 情诗):

> Two petals of leaf-like cyan mountains,
> Clip half a cherry-like red sun;

---

[50] Ibid., 15.

I give my souls to joy,
Fire-wise kiss this water-like lively light.

两瓣树叶般的青山，
夹着半颗樱桃般的红阳；
我将魂灵交给快乐，
火样吻这水般活泼的光。[51]

Here the mountains and the sun are compared to leaves and cherry. The gathering of "two petals" and "cherry-like red" exudes a strong morphological denotation of female genitals. The act that "I" kiss the "water-like" light discharged by a "cherry-like" sun could be interpreted as an act of cunnilingus. The juxtaposition of phrases "fire-wise" and "water-like" is again a highly playful dialectic swing that is reminiscent of the swing between "slut and virgin" in "Peony". This kind of sexual s(t)imulation is also played with in a poem entitled "I Dare Not Go to Heaven" (Wo bugan shangtian 我不敢上天):

Though I've smelled the scent of flowers,
And I've tasted stories of sweetness,
But the scary thing is the tenderest two petals,
That make me immersed in it all my life.

虽然我已经闻过了花香，
甜蜜的故事我也曾品尝，
但是可怕那最嫩的两瓣，
尽叫我一世在里面荡漾。[52]

The terms "tasted", "two petals" and "immersed" once again give a hint of female genitals. "Scent", "sweetness" and "tenderest" correspond to the sense of smell, taste and touch, of flowers and the woman's body. With the interweaving of senses in the texture of the poem, the flowers and the female sexual organs are united as one, and the interaction between the poetic voice and the union again gives an allusion to cunnilingus.

As a reader would very often take the role of "I" when reading a poem, he/she would enter the erotic scenario and be stimulated through the simulation of sex. As the flower is considered by Shao as an incarnation of music, the flower-woman's body is rendered by him as an instrument to reach the biunivocal

---

[51] Ibid., 37.
[52] Ibid., 155.

condition of music and sexual ecstasy. In the next section, I will examine the texts that might have influenced Shao's unique equation of music with sexual ecstasy.

2.2.3 Garden, sexual ecstasy and possible biblical influence

Flower petals frequently occur in Shao's poetic works and he often implicitly compares them to female sexual organs. The fall of petals is therefore linked to the loss of sexual consummation, which is evident in a poem called "Love's Debt" (Qingzang 情赃):

> Like two, three pieces of white rose petals,
> Tender and smooth, they might dizzy your eyes:
> This piece has a billion tons of advice, relief;
> That piece has a billion tons of jealousy, malice;
>
> And this one last piece has broken long ago,
> Tears wet it, or tongues licked it?
> You can have it back, I'm afraid white petals'll turn yellow,
> They've left you, left the fountain of life.

> 像是白蔷薇的花瓣儿两片三片，
> 又嫩又滑的，留心看晕了你的眼：
> 这一片有几千万斤的劝告，安慰；
> 那一片有几千万斤的醋意，怨嗔；
>
> 再有最后的一片，早已残缺不全，
> 是泪儿湿化了，还是经了舌儿舔?
> 啊，还了你吧，我怕白花瓣会变黄，
> 他们已离了你，离了生命的源泉。[53]

"Tongues licked it" again cues cunnilingus. And as the petals have broken, they could no longer be licked or be engaged in other sexual activities. Here "you" refers to the flower and also the female sexual organs. The flower is "the fountain of life" for petals, and the female sexual organs are "the fountain of life" in the sense of reproduction. As sexual consummation with the flower-woman is equated by Shao with the condition of music in poetry, this "fountain of life" is also the fountain for the musical condition in poetry. To the petals, the supplier of life is the organicity of the flower that organizes the petals in the

---

[53] Ibid., 168.

entirety. The petals fall and fall out of the organic entirety of the flower, hence leaving the fountain of life, the musical condition of poetry. However, in a poem entitled "Fallen Petals" (Duoluo de huaban 堕落的花瓣), the dynamic of flower and petals functions differently:

> Fallen petals
> Stick to your
> Cyan lapels,
> Smelling good.
>
> Beauty's devil;
> Loving you,
> She'll taint you,
> For sure.
>
> 堕落的花瓣
> 贴紧你
> 青衫的衣襟，
> 怪香的。
>
> 美人是魔鬼；
> 爱了你，
> 她总沾污你，
> 一定的。[54]

This poem progresses in a slow, roving pace, which mimics the falling of petals, or simply, the gesture of falling. Here a woman, a devil and some petals are conglomerated. The act that petals fall on the cyan lapels is paired up with the act that a woman engages in sexual activities with the wearer of the cyan lapels; in this sense, the falling petals and the woman are tangled. And as "she" is in the second stanza the initiator of the act of tainting, it could be deduced that "she" is the beauty equated with a devil; hence the woman and the devil are tangled. The devil is a religious embodiment of the fallen; through the texture of "fall" the devil and the fallen petals are tangled, thus completing an organic, self-contained circle of significance. It should be noted that the texture of "fall" dwells on the underpinning of Christian allusions. Though Shao graduated from St John's, a famous episcopal high school in Shanghai before he headed to Cambridge, it is difficult to make a definite deduction on his religious views.

---

[54] Ibid., 19.

That being said, what could be affirmed is that there are indeed many poems dealing with Christianity in his oeuvre. In "Xunmei's Dream" he writes:

> In a poet's flesh there's no seedling of filth,
> The embryo is for sure a crystal pure,
> An emerald if in love with green leaves,
> Bright like coral if with red flowers:
> So then God has a second son,
> In the clean fresh church a new Bible is set.

> 诗人的肉里没有污浊的秧苗，
> 胚胎当然是一块纯粹的水晶，
> 将来爱上了绿叶便变成翡翠，
> 爱上了红花便像珊瑚般妍明：
> 于是上帝又有了第二个儿子，
> 清净的庙堂里重换一本圣经。[55]

Here "God", "church" and "Bible" are juxtaposed with "green leaves" and "red flowers". The gathering of Christian terms and plants often appears in Shao's poems.

He writes in "The Song of Man" (Renqu 人曲): "[…]God's wish/ As delicate as flowers and leaves growing on twigs" ("[…]上帝的愿/ 巧得像花叶长上树枝").[56] A more elaborate allusion to Christianity would be a long poem entitled "The Poem of Heaven" (Tiantang zhi shi 天堂之什), which retells the story of Eden with an almost iconoclastic emphasis on garden(ing). He writes in the second canto:

> In the green grass an apple tree
> Blossoms.
> God!
> You're in love!
> You breathe a breeze like whisper;
> You cry some dew like the tears of love.
> The flower smiles;
> Like a virgin who loves her first lover
> Loves you,
> She fruits,

---

[55] Ibid., 131.
[56] Ibid., 204.

Ah it's your ability!
God!

青草丛里的苹果树
开了花了。
上帝！
你爱了！
你吐着絮语的和风；
你流着情泪的轻露。
花笑了；
像处女爱第一个情人
一般地爱你了，
结果了，
是你的能力吓！
上帝！ [57]

Here the Bible is tangled with the organic chronicle of a plant-woman. She is concurrently the flower of an apple tree, and a virgin who loves her first lover. The two mechanisms/organisms that interpret the cause of a new life are here conglomerated. It is God's ability that gives life to a fruit; and it is due to the organic copulation that a fruit is conceived. What is noteworthy here is the copulation of Christianity and horticulture. God breathes an intimate whisper-like breeze and sheds some tears-of-love-resembling dew in order to nurture his lover, a plant-woman. The poem goes on:

The flower fruits,
Gets big,
Swells,
Fulfills,
You laugh;
Laugh so that your saliva fountains,
Thunders and rain,
The fruit drops.
It's your effort!
God!

---

[57] Ibid., 53-54.

花结果了，
大了，
膨胀了，
圆满了，
你笑了；
笑得瀺唾喷了，
雷吓雨吓，
果子落下来了。
是你的功劳吓！
上帝!⁵⁸

The conceived plant-woman reaches a point of delivery. And a fruit is born/made. God in this text takes on a role that is similar to a poet (and one could certainly say it the other way around). He creates life inside the realm of the given text, but the life created has its organic growth pattern and would outgrow any univocal inference inflicted by the creator. The text continues and shifts the focus from the plant-woman to the fruit, or, the poem, since the discursive world of God could be substituted with that of a poet:

> The fruit drops,
> The fruit of freedom,
> He has no restraints at all;
> A contented fruit,
> Wherever he drops,
> He stays there at ease,
> He's not wishing for feet,
> Not wishing for having feet
> To run into your heaven!
> It's the fruit you caused!
> God!
>
> It's the fruit you caused,
> You put him aside.
> He rots,
> He leaves his roots and dies,
> The roots sprout again,
> The sprouts grow into a tree again,
> The tree blossoms again,

---

⁵⁸ Ibid., 54.

You love again,
The flower fruits again;

果子落下来了，
是自由的果子吓，
他没有一切的束缚；
是知足的果子吓，
他落下在那里，
便安心在那里，
他不求生脚，
更不求生了脚，
跑上你的天堂！
这是你造成的果子吓！
上帝！

是你造成的果子吓，
你弃着不理。
他腐烂了，
他留下了根而化了，
根发芽了，
芽又成树了，
树又开花了，
你又爱了，
花又结果了;[59]

The fruit/poem is caused by the God/poet. But after being caused it is independent of the initiator of the cause and it starts to gain creative freedom, which has no restraints in its multiplicity of possibilities. It rots; it dies; yet the story of a fallen fruit does not stop here. The organicity of it does not vanish into nothingness. The corpse of it becomes the source of nutrition for sprouts that are about to sprout. Life does not stop for a change of vessel; it continues in different forms. In the following stanzas, the repeated life circle of an apple flower/fruit leads to the slow accumulation of apple trees and eventually the occurrence of an exuberant apple garden. The poem then goes on to the biblical story that gathers Satan, Adam and Eve. The end of the poem is staged in the apple garden:

---

[59] Ibid., 55.

Softly he opens the garden gate,
Sneakily hides in the shades;
Sings songs that please ears,
Reads poems that shake hearts.
Adam hears that.
Eve hears that.
"Ah I'm burning here."
Adam points to his face.
"Ah I'm beating here."
Eve points to her heart.
Now it's Satan's job!
God!

They follow the songs and poems,
Into the gate.
As two that've eaten no fruits,
The colors of the fruits have wet their tongues.
They taste and try!
Mutually taste and try!
Now they know!
But before they know
Joy sorrow shame and everything,
They first know love!
God!

他轻轻地开了园门,
偷偷地藏入树荫;
唱着入耳的歌,
吟着动心的诗。
亚当听得了。
夏娃听得了。
"啊我此地在烧。"
亚当指着脸。
"啊我此地在跳。"
夏娃指着心。
这是杀旦的工作了!
上帝!

他俩寻着歌诗,
进了园门。

啊没吃到果子的人，
果子的颜色已使他们生津。
他俩尝着试着！
相相地尝试着！
他俩知道了！
但是他俩在知道
快乐悲苦羞耻一切以前，
先知道了爱！
上帝![60]

The garden gathering starts with the lure of Satan; the baits are songs and poems. Satan here is not only the embodiment of poetic freedom, which challenges the order imposed by God, but also the incarnation of the fall: the fall into sexual consummation and the condition of music in poetry. By organically consuming the fruits, Adam and Eve gain the organic complexity of senses and become lives independent from the creation of God. The organicized Adam and Eve remain in the cultivated garden, and the poem ends here, giving the poem itself the entirety. This, in analogy to the fallen petals discussed in "Fallen Petals", is a fall into organicity. Here Satan does what the devil in "Fallen Petals" does: he makes…fall. The organicity of him is not just a property, but an ability. Earlier in "The Poem of Heaven", Satan is said to have the capability to metamorphose into various animals:

> He can walk on the wall like a snake
> He can dash in the mountains like a horse
> He can swim in the heart of water like a fish;
> He can soar in the sky like a bird

> 他会像蛇般在墙上行走
> 他会像马般在山中狂奔
> 他会像鱼般在水心游泳；
> 他会像鸟般在天空飞腾[61]

Interestingly, the association of Satan and a snake is also played with in a poem titled "Snake" (She 蛇), where an animal-woman, instead of the plant-women that frequent Shao's other poems, appears to have sex with the poetic voice:

---

[60] Ibid., 59-60.
[61] Ibid., 57.

Under the stairs of a palace, on the tiles of a temple,
You let drop the most slender of you—

Like a woman's half-loosened belt
Waiting for men's shaky bravery.

在宫殿的阶下，在庙宇的瓦上，
你垂下你最柔嫩的一段—

好像是女人半松的裤带
在等待着男性的颤抖的勇敢。 [62]

The Satan/snake and the woman are here merged as one. This satanic seductive snake is tangled with a woman through its resemblance to her "half-loosened belt". The snake-woman's slenderness and the hint of "men's shaky bravery" is again cueing an act of penetrative sex. The poem goes on:

I don't know your blood-red biforked tongue
Is to sting which side of my lips?
They are ready, ready for
The double exultation in this one hour!

I can't forget your uncatchable slipperiness
Has polished how many folded bamboo joints:
I know there's pain in comfort,
And I know there's fire in cold ice.

I wish you use the rest of you
To hoop tight my unhoopable body,
When the sound of the bell sneaks in a cloudy room's gauze netting,
And warmth crawls over a cold palace's thin stitched-sheets!

我不懂你血红的叉分的舌尖
要刺痛我那一边的嘴唇?
他们都准备着了，准备着
这同一个时辰里双倍的欢欣!

---

[62] Ibid., 165.

我忘不了你那捉不住的油滑
磨光了多少重叠的竹节:
我知道了舒服里有伤痛,
我更知道了冰冷里还有火炽。

啊,但愿你再把你剩下的一段
来箍紧我箍不紧的身体,
当钟声偷进云房的纱帐,
温暖爬满了冷宫稀薄的绣被![63]

Here one could summarize the snake-woman's texture in three alliterating words: sting, slippery and sleaziness. The stinging on lips, the polishing of bamboo joints and the hooping of the body are three acts of bodily contact. The biforked tongue's stinging on two sides of lips is a playful double kiss. It is a kiss that consists of two concurrent kisses. The polishing of bamboo joints could be seen as a metamorphosing mimic of a penis' organic engagement with a vagina. And in this mimic, both ends are valid in the presentation of their respective dynamic. The hooping of an unhoopable body is an attempt to conglomerate two bodies, and to unite the dichotomy of you and I, hoop and un-hoop, pain and comfort, fire and ice, the warmth and the cold of the palace. Interestingly, this snake-woman also appears in a poem called "Z's Smile" (Z de xiao Z 的笑):

I know your heart, cold fire,
Like a burning smoking icehouse.
You lower your head and smile, you turn your back to me and smile,
Your snake waist's curve reveals the love that loves me.

我知道了你的心,冷的火炎,
像在燃烧的冒着烟的冰窖。
你低了头笑,你有意将背心向了我而笑,
啊,你蛇腰上的曲线已露着爱我的爱了。 [64]

Here the snake-woman has the same organic playfulness as the one in "Snake". The love between "I" and the snake-woman, with the similar wrestle of dichotomy such as cold fire and burning icehouse, is again ambiguous, biunivocal and undecodable. The ambiguity of this snake-woman is also

---

[63] Ibid., 166.
[64] Ibid., 9.

played with in a poem entitled "Madonna Mia".⁶⁵ This poem is about a woman who has pomegranate lips, and is capable of becoming a multiplicity of things:

> Ah moon-like eyebrows and starry teeth,
> You enchant the world, the world's enchanted;
> Ah when you open your pomegranate lips,
> Many with souls, lose their souls.
>
> You're Xishi,⁶⁶ you're a virgin washing muslin,
> You're a serpent, you're a monster that kills:
> Life consumes you so you consume life,
> Ah they are willing, willing to sacrifice for you.
>
> Why fear, a desire sharp as a bee's sting?
> Stings the heart of happiness, flooding blood?
> With you I'll kiss and kiss,
> I'll forget after tonight, there is tomorrow.

> 啊，月儿样的眉星般的牙齿，
> 你迷尽了一世，一世为你痴；
> 啊，当你开闭你石榴色的嘴唇，
> 多少有灵魂的，便失去了灵魂。
>
> 你是西施，你是浣纱的处女，
> 你是毒蟒，你是杀人的妖异：
> 生命消受你，你便来消受生命，
> 啊，他们愿意的愿意为你牺牲。
>
> 怕甚，像蜂针般尖利的欲情？
> 刺着快乐的心儿，流血涔涔？
> 有了你，我便要一吻而再吻，
> 我将忘却天夜之后，复有天明。⁶⁷

Here this pomegranate-woman also becomes a serpent. What comes out of the act of becoming is a pomegranate-serpent-woman, an unidentifiable hybrid of plant and animal. This body could be seen as the entirety of the garden; it is the

---

⁶⁵ This is the original title of the poem.
⁶⁶ A woman of extreme beauty that occurs in ancient Chinese folktales.
⁶⁷ Ibid., 6.

ultimate organic body that unifies the multiplicity of different framing organisms. "Life consumes you so you consume life." In the act of mutual consumption, this garden body becomes the equivalence of life. Hence the garden is in its entirety the life of the poem, which is the utmost insuperable organism that organizes the body. "I'll forget after tonight, there is tomorrow." The life of the poem stays in the entirety of the garden, the tonight of its life.

However, beside the fall into sexual ecstasy, there is another kind of fall, the fall of unfertilized flowers resulting from the lack of sexual consummation. In a poem called "Yesterday's Garden" (Zuori de yuanzi 昨日的园子) Shao presents a desolate lifeless garden:

> There's a garden of yesterday,
> The cyan leaves are yellowed;
> The lively flowers are withered;
> The brisk birds are dead.
>
> And a couple of lovers,
> Hugging and kissing;
> With no breath and no sound,
> They're God's loved offsprings.

> 这里有个昨日的园子，
> 青的叶儿是黄了的；
> 鲜的花儿是谢了的；
> 活泼的鸟儿是死了的。
>
> 还有一对有情的人儿，
> 相相地拥抱了亲吻；
> 没有气吓也没有声，
> 啊他们是上帝的爱儿。[68]

The fall of flowers without sexual consummation denotes an act of fruitless withering, the loss of life for the garden. The couple, presumably alluding to Adam and Eve, are breathless and engaged in a petrified posture of hugging and kissing. They are "with no breath", dead and in lack of sexual consummation. Note that there is "no sound" produced in this frozen posture: the condition of

---

[68] Ibid., 13-14.

music in poetry, which Shao associates with sexual consummation, is not achieved.

Shao's idea of the garden and the fall of the flower woman suggests a biblical influence. This influence is synthesized into his unique rendering of the horticulture of musical sisters, that is, the instrumentalization of a woman's body so as to achieve a condition of music in poetry.

2.2.4 The instrumentalisation of woman's body

As the flower-women in the previous excerpts suggest, Shao regards the woman's body as a musical instrument to reach the condition of music in poetry. In an episode of *Friday on Poetry* entitled "The Production of Poetry" (Shi de chansheng 诗的产生) he maintains that "A poet should create poetry with the same effort that God creates the universe" ("一个诗人应当用上帝创造宇宙的苦心来创造诗").[69] This is reminiscent of the biblical influence that I talked about in the previous section. He writes:

> I think there are no more accurate ways to describe this experience than a woman's labor. An idea of a poem comes like a sperm; its minuteness cannot be seen by eyes. But it has its presence; it has its life; it then stays in the womb. The mother at first has no idea; she has no clue she'd be using her blood to nurture the life of this embryo. The embryo gradually grows—it gets blood, it gets flesh, it gets skin and bones—it grows to an extent that the mother has to give birth. Hence an individual life owns its existence.
>
> 我以为用女人的生产来描写这种经验是再确当也没有的了。诗兴来时正像是精子，它的微细不是眼睛所能看得见的。但是它有它的存在，它有它的生命，它从此便留存在子宫里了。做母亲的起初完全不知道，她更不知道她此后便用自己的血液在滋养着这胚胎的生命。胚胎渐渐长大了，— 有了血，有了肉，也有皮也有骨头 — 长大到母亲不由自主地非生产不可。于是一个单独的生命便有了自己的存在。[70]

Here the composition of a poem is compared to the organic process of a woman's conception, gestation and delivery. An embryo is the primordial state of a poem that starts to consist of entities resembling organic tissues: blood, flesh, skin and bones. Texture to a poem is exactly what tissues are to a body.

---

[69] Originally published in *China-US Daily* on Feb 24, 1939. Here quoted from a reprint in *Shi tansuo* 诗探索 [Poetry Exploration] 2010 volume 1, 29.
[70] Ibid.

When this embryo has grown to a state of full constitution, the poet would have to deliver it. And after the delivery, the poem as a living thing is independent of the poet.

However, in the entire process, the role of the egg is ignored as Shao states that a sperm comes to the womb and an embryo is formed, which is unscientific. Apart from the negligence of the egg, in Shao's notion of gestation, there is also a common misunderstanding about which entity comes first. Bordo states that "on most occasions when fertilization occurs it is actually the egg that travels to rendezvous with sperm that have been lolling around, for as much as three days, waiting for her to arrive".[71] With the negligence and misunderstanding, Shao describes the woman's body purely as a recipient of sperm and only a carrier of an embryo that develops solely from a sperm. This idea is reminiscent of the theories and practices in what Bordo describes as the "gynophobic century" of 1550-1650. She writes:

> It was not only in practice that women were being denied an active role in the processes of conception and birth. Mechanist reproductive theory as well had "happily" (as Easlea sarcastically puts it) made it "no longer necessary to refer to any women" at all in its descriptions of conception and gestation. Denied even her limited, traditional Aristotelian role of supplying (living) menstrual material, the woman becomes instead the mere container for the temporary housing and incubation of already formed human beings, originally placed in Adam's semen by God and parcelled out, over the ages, to all his male descendants. The specifics of mechanistic reproductive theory are a microcosmic recapitulation of the mechanistic vision itself, within which God the father is the sole creative, formative principle in the cosmos.[72]

The biblical influence and the place of "God the father" in Shao's conception of reproduction have been examined in the previous section. In this conception, the agency of the woman is denied by Shao and the woman's body is instrumentalized as a tool to get a final product—a baby, or in the metaphor of Shao's excerpt, a poem.

---

[71] Susan Bordo, *Unbearable Weight: Feminism, Western Culture, and the Body* (Berkeley: University of California Press, 1993), 13.
[72] Susan Bordo, "The Cartesian Masculinization of Thought", *Signs* 1986, vol. 11, no. 3: 453. The essay was later revised and anthologized in her book *The Flight to Objectivity: Essays on Cartesianism and Culture* (New York: SUNY Press, 1987).

Strangely, some critics claim that the rendering of woman's body in Shao's poetry shows his laudation for women. Chen Mengjia 陈梦家,[73] a contemporary of Shao who was associated with the Crescent Moon Society, considers Shao's poems to be "the weather of a soft charming March of spring, voluptuous like a compliments-worthy voluptuous woman whose silken bearing is adorable" ("邵洵美的诗，是柔美的迷人的春三月的天气，艳丽如一个应该赞美的艳丽的女人，只是那缱绻是十分可爱的").[74] The repetition of the term "voluptuous" as well as the diction of "silken bearing" puts emphasis on the sexual features of a woman, thus downgrading the woman to merely an object for the male gaze. The term "compliments-worthy" shows a condescending attitude, as if the worth of a woman depends on her sexual features. As for those who seem to criticize the rendering of the woman's body in Shao's poetry, it appears that their focus is conventionally moralistic. One of the most famous attacks on Shao in Republican China was a review signed with the pseudonym Sun Meiseng 孙梅僧 in the journal *Bitter Tea* (Kucha 苦茶), which bombards Shao in a way similar to the one Robert Buchanan launched on "the fleshly school" of Dante Rossetti and Swinburne in 1871.[75] It pivots on the criticism that Shao's poems are way too fleshy and full of vulgar, immoral accumulation of words like "flesh" (rou 肉), "kiss" (wen 吻), "lips" (chun 唇), "tongue" (she 舌) and "virgin" (chunü 处女).[76] Besides, at the time many left-wing critics such as Qu Qiubai 瞿秋白[77] dismiss works like Shao's as "pornography" ("色情").[78] Xie Zhixi 解志熙, a contemporary scholar, affirms this statement by claiming that in Shao's poems "there are only barefaced

---

[73] Chen Mengjia (1911-1966) was a poet and art critic. His famous works include the poetry collections *Mengjia's Poems* (Mengjia shiji 梦家诗集) (1931) and *Iron Horse* (Tiema ji 铁马集) (1934).
[74] Here quoted from *A Selection of Works and Critical Reception of Sphinx Club*, 291.
[75] Robert Buchanan, "The Fleshly School of Poetry: Mr. D. G. Rossetti", *The Contemporary Review* volume 18 August-November 1871, under the nom de plume of Thomas Maitland.
[76] Sun Meiseng 孙梅僧, *Bitter Tea* volume 4 (1928). Here quoted from *A Selection of Works and Critical Reception of Sphinx Club*, 349.
[77] Qu Qiubai (1899-1935) was a writer and one of the early leaders of the Chinese Communist Party. His most notable work is *In the Capital of Red* (Chidu xinshi 赤都心史), a collection of causeries about his visit of Moscow in 1920.
[78] Qu Qiubai 瞿秋白, *Maoyang de shiren* 猫样的诗人 [Cat-like Poets], in *Qu qiubai wenji* 瞿秋白文集 [Works of Qu Qiubai] (Beijing: Renmin wenxue chubanshe, 1953), 270.

sensory desires and the discharge of life's instincts" ("只有赤裸裸的感官欲望和生命本能的宣泄").[79] He writes:

> What has been presented to the readers is a "visual feast" that consists of women's "red lips", "tongue tip", "cleavage", "belly", "snaky waist" or even "genitals", while the only theme is to encourage people to have fun in the bitterness of a depraved world.
>
> 呈现给读者的是有所谓女性的"红唇"、"舌尖"、"乳壕"、"肚脐"、"蛇腰"直至女性的"下体"所组成的"视觉之盛宴",而唯一的主题即是鼓励人们在颓废的人间苦中及时行乐。[80]

It is true that the representations of women in Shao's poems often focus on their cleavage and hips. If one tries to draw the image of such a woman, it will look very similar to the nineteenth-century hourglass figure, which in Bordo's words is "an intelligible symbolic form, representing a domestic, sexualized ideal of femininity."[81] However, these cited male critics from the republican era to the current age do not see what is truly problematic. They notice Shao's exploitation of the woman's body, but their arguments only revolve around a judgement on morals and its wrestling with sexual instincts. Shao responds by questioning the validity of such criticism that dwells on the underpinning of morals: "Beauty has no boundary. We can't say that Jesus' virgin mother can be deemed beautiful yet a voluptuous Salome can't" ("'美'是没有界限的。并不是说耶稣的处女母亲可称'美',而妖媚的莎乐美便不能称'美'").[82] Here two female bodies are named to illustrate beauty's irrelevance to morals; to Shao beauty is almost a synonym of female body, while moral or immoral are simply adjectives that derive their meanings from the intertextual chains to which they have simultaneously contributed. The stripping of the female body is at the same the exposure of the hypocrisy that lies behind words like moral or immoral. In another poem titled "Sweet Dream" (Tianmi meng 甜蜜梦) morals and the act of disrobing are again paired up:

---

[79] Xie Zhixi 解志熙, *Meide pianzhi* 美的偏至 [The Extreme of Beauty] (Shanghai: Shanghai wenxue chubanshe, 1997), 229.
[80] Ibid., 229-230.
[81] Susan Bordo, *Unbearable Weight: Feminism, Western Culture, and the Body* (Berkeley: University of California Press, 1993), 181.
[82] Shao, "About the Criticism on Flower-like Evil" (Guanyu huayiban de zuie de piping 关于《花一般的罪恶》的批评), *Collected Works of Shao Xunmei*, 150.

Lovely, scary, proudhearted,
Virgins' tongues' tips, geckos' tails.
I don't know, could you tell me,
If there's pleasure in four lips?

Ah a rosy ivory bed,
This sweet dream keeps busy my soul:
I'm a believer of evil:
I want to see world-longing nuns undress.

可爱的，可怕的，可骄人的，
处女的舌尖，壁虎的尾巴。
我不懂，你可能对我说吗，
四片的嘴唇中真有愉快？

啊，玫瑰色，象牙色的一床，
这种的甜蜜梦，害我魂忙：
我是个罪恶底忠实信徒：
我想看思凡的尼姑卸装。[83]

"A believer of evil" is a witness of the polarity that underlies the construction of the term moral, which cannot stand alone meaningfully without its very dichotomy. In this sense, a believer of evil is a believer of moral. When a world-longing nun undresses, morals are stripped to their core. Virgins' tongues and lips, beautifully displayed and displaying beauty, are all that matter to Shao. This strong impulse to negate morals' imposition on poetry is also exemplified in "Our Queen" (Women de huanghou 我们的皇后):

Why are you bittered for people's buzz?
It's time to do your belly dance
There're no saints unlustful in the pure sinned world
Queen, our queen

You wolfy foxy cute lady
You've for sure used your lips to kiss
Your scent of mouth has poisoned us all
Queen, our queen

---

[83] Shao, *Poetic Works of Shao Xunmei*, 120.

Forget prophets brothers and fathers
Men'll all bow down to your pubes
Ah save us from morals
Queen, our queen

为甚你因人们的指摘而愤恨?
这正是你跳你肚脐舞的时辰,
净罪界中没有不好色的圣人。
皇后,我们的皇后。

你这似狼似狐的可爱的妇人,
你已毋庸将你的嘴唇来亲吻,
你口齿的芬芳便毒尽了众生。
皇后,我们的皇后。

管什么先知管什么哥哥爸爸?
男性的都将向你的下体膜拜。
啊将我们从道德中救出来吧。
皇后,我们的皇后。[84]

Here belly, lips, mouth are amorously presented, in juxtaposition with "no saints unlustful" and "the pure sinned world": it is a world where moral hypocrisy has been banished and what is left to worship is a clean stripped female body. The poem itself resembles a rite of worship as "queen, our queen" occurs as an almost chant-like refrain. It is enchanting, especially when the prayer is said: "Save us from morals". When the previously-mentioned critics condemn Shao for having no morals, it is true. It is true not in the sense that Shao is immoral, but in the sense that he does not believe in the equation of moral value with poetic value. Those critics do not realize that there is a real horror behind what they regard as Shao's moral incorrectness—that lust is not for lust's sake, and that Shao negates the agency of woman and instrumentalizes woman's body so as to reach a condition of music in poetry. This is most evident in a poem entitled "Xunmei's Dream" (Xunmei de meng 洵美的梦):

From red hot green hot lotus blossoms
A fervid dream, she holds tight my soul.

---

[84] Ibid., 65.

Shao, Sitwell and "the sister of horticulture"

She's light as cloud, I wonder why she
Doesn't fly to the sky or hide at the pool's heart?
I remember she's brought gifts of hope
To chill holes on quilts, and desire
To startle the most sleepless virgin,
So she hears from dog bark to cock crow.

从滚红滚绿的荷花里开出了
热温温的梦，她偎紧我的魂灵。
她轻得像云，我奇怪她为什么
不飞上天顶或是深躲在潭心?
我记得她曾带了满望的礼物
蹑进失意的被洞，又带了私情
去惊醒了最不容易睡的处女，
害她从悠长的狗吠听到鸡鸣。[85]

Note the flower symbol "red hot green hot lotus". Though Shao's women in poetry are not always presented as flower-women, in most cases, they would be accompanied with flowers. The lotus, the reproductive organ of the lotus plant, yields "a fervid dream". As this dream is given a female pronoun, a woman's body that shares the texture of dream is presented. Here this dream is to Shao female and the female is to Shao dreamy. The terms "holes on quilts" and "the most sleepless virgin" give this dreamy body a strong sexual indication. The lines go on:

But she's not often at my place, I guess
She's not sure about my bedtime.
I'd like to sleep the sun's company, I hope
Nightingales won't disturb my sleepy mind
Perhaps at this moment of leisure I will
Go through a door where flowers all can
Turn their various colors into songs,
Into poems, to sing soft a morning of spring.

但是我这里她不常来到，想是
她猜不准我夜晚上床的时辰。
我爱让太阳伴了我睡，我希望
夜莺不再搅扰我倦眠的心神

---

[85] Shao, *Poetic Works of Shao Xunmei,* 130.

也许乘了这一忽的空闲，我会
走进一个园门，那里的花都能
把他们的色彩芬芳编成歌曲，
做成诗，去唱软那春天的早晨。 [86]

"Not often at my place" suggests a lack of dream in the poetic voice. And "this moment of leisure" denotes the moment of successful commencement of dreaming, and it could also be interpreted as an allusion to sex. In this sense, the coming of "she" to me signifies at the same time dreaming and having sex with the woman. Note that in the text what follows from "this moment of leisure" is to "Go through a door where flowers all can/ Turn their various colors into songs, / Into poems". Here "door" could be deduced as Shao's symbol for female genitals and "go through a door" leads to an act of entering into the female body. However, the word "door" also denotes that Shao regards it only as a passage, a means to somewhere behind the "door". The poetic voice is to go right through the woman's body, to a place with songs. The body is therefore instrumentalized as a means to get to an end. This end is "Go through a door where flowers all can/ Turn their various colors into songs, / Into poems", a condition of music reached in poetry.

But the dream does not stop here. In the following lines, Shao states clearly that he treats the woman's body as an instrument:

> Even with one string left, I believe
> She's still to play her chopping tunes,
> (In the chopping there's fuller touching)
> No matter how you lock your ears,
> There's fire in this string, she will
> Fry you, boil you, burn your iron's hardness.
> Then I will for sure pluck her,
> To help heaven impregnate her poet.

就算是剩下了一根弦，我相信
她还是要弹出她屑碎的迷音，
(这屑碎里面有更完全的缠绵)
任你能锁住了你的耳朵不听，
怎奈这一根弦里有火，她竟会
煎你，熬你，烧烂你铁石的坚硬。

---

[86] Ibid., 130-131.

那时我一定要把她摘采下来，
帮助了天去为她的诗人怀孕。[87]

The dream, the woman's body plays the remaining string of an instrument unnamed. "In the chopping there's fuller touching" designates that the sense of bodily touching, the touching of the string and the metaphorical sense of touching (moved) are here merged. As the three kinds of touching have conglomerated, in sync, the female body (bodily touching), the string (touching of the string) and the signification (touched) are united as one. The woman is concurrently the musical instrument and the poem. This trinity of body, music and signification is made more explicit in a poem entitled "Woman" (Nüren 女人):

> I respect you, woman, I respect you like
> I respect a verset of Tang—
> You use mild even and crispy oblique tones,
> To tie up my words and phrases.

> 我敬重你，女人，我敬重你正像
> 我敬重一首唐人的小诗——
> 你用温润的平声干脆的仄声，
> 来捆缚住我的一句一字。[88]

In this stanza, a woman is connected to a verset of Tang through the rhizome of poesis. The woman's body, with the ability to utter even and oblique tones, is compared to the textual body of the verset which could yield even and oblique tones when read. It is hard to tell whether the verset is the simulacrum of the woman or the woman the simulacrum of the verset. Both bodies could serve as musical instruments and vessels of meaning. It could be seen that there are two separate bodies present in this stanza and each of them makes music and delivers a univocal message. Or, it could be seen that there is only one music-making biunivocal body, which is the conglomeration of woman-verset. It should be noted that this is not the only occasion where Shao compares a woman to a poem. In a poem entitled "Who Do You Think I Am" (Ni yiwei wo shi shenmeren 你以为我是什么人) Shao remarks that "I love women for they are

---

[87] Ibid., 131.
[88] Ibid., 133.

all poetry" ("我爱女人为了她们都是诗").[89] A woman's body is to Shao a means, a sensing-cyborg through which he observes the world. He writes:

> Am I mistaking soap bubbles for rainbows,
> Cat meows for the laughters of spring,
> Tadpoles for women's eyes?
> I don't know, I don't know at all,
> You have to ask the poet who tells no lies.

> 是不是把肥皂泡当作了虹,
> 把猫叫当作了春的笑声,
> 把蝌蚪当作了女人的眼睛?
> 我不知道, 我全不知道,
> 你得去问那个不说诳的诗人。[90]

Tadpoles could be seen as women's eyes due to their morphological resemblance. And as women are to him poetry, women's eyes/the tadpoles are certainly poetic. Yet beside things that bear easily perceptible morphological similarities and hence could be obviously interpreted with the flesh of woman, Shao manages to see a woman in rather *womanless* places. In a poem entitled "Horror" (Kongbu 恐怖) a landscape is cleaved to a woman's body:

> In my heart still lingers your shadow,
> Yet on my mouth fades your lipstick,
> The sun's red light has gathered on the mountain's shoulder,
> The moment to light is again coming.

> In my nose is but your filthy odor,
> Before my eyes is your blood-like sinned skin,
> The sun's red light has gathered on the mountain's shoulder,
> The moment to light is again coming.

> 我底心中还留着你底小影,
> 我底嘴上却消了你底唇痕,
> 太阳的红光已聚在山肩了,
> 啊那上灯的时分又要到了。

---

[89] Ibid., 151.
[90] Ibid., 152.

鼻里不绝你那醒醒的香气，
眼前总有你那血般的罪肌，
太阳的红光已聚在山肩了，
啊那上灯的时分又要到了。[91]

This woman is everything; her body stretches out extensively and gets tangled with the perception of a landscape in twilight. She is all that the poetic voice smells, sees and touches, sensualizing the world that the poetic voice observes. One might question whether there is a woman's full, univocal body present or merely a hallucinatory shadow that cues an analogy to "woman".

Shao's claimed "respect" for women is not a respect but a posture that salutes something outside the woman. In "Xunmei's Dream" the poetic voice states that he will pluck her to "impregnate her poet". This resonates with Shao's idea of a conception with no egg involved, which I have discussed earlier in the chapter. Shao regards woman's body only as a carrier, an instrument in poetry to yield a condition of music. The significance of this condition of music is equated by Shao with a sexual ecstasy gained from the woman's body.

This unique equation does not simply spring from the influence of Sitwell's conception of "the sister of horticulture" and "texture", or Qian's and Weng's ideas of Jili. In the previous chapter, I have stated that Shao, like Swinburne, regards Sappho as the embodiment of poetry, and the very conception of embodiment itself creates a sense of body for poetry. And as Sappho's gender is already given to Shao as female, he holds the idea that Sappho, a woman, embodies poetry. Poetry is to him not only personified, but also exclusively gendered as female. It is on the basis of this that Shao gradually synthesizes the influence of Sitwell, Qian and Weng, and comes to engraft Sappho, the female body of poetry, onto the flower, the incarnation of music. In this way, Shao creates a musical instrument, the playing of which will create a condition of music in poetry.

It should be noted that in the previous chapter, Sappho as the nightingale-woman is considered by Shao as a performer. Here the flower-woman, the flower-Sappho I should say, is downgraded by Shao to an instrument. And the playing of the instrument is to him a synonym of playing the body, which is having sex with the female body. Though Shao abolishes the concerns of morals in his unique equation, his rendering still poses a detriment to a woman's agency by objectifying a woman's body on an ontological level that might be far more dangerous than morals. However, Shao's poetics is never a closed system. As time goes by, new influence on Shao gradually breaks into this equation and

---

[91] Ibid., 18.

reshapes his poetics on the body and gender of poetry and music, as well as how the condition of music can be achieved in poetry.

Chapter 3

Shao, Moore and the idea of pure poetry

3.1 Shao and Moore in dialogue

3.1.1 Shao's correspondence with Moore

Among the writers that influenced Shao, George Moore is the one with whom he had actual, and frequent correspondence. In August 1928 Shao published an article entitled "Pure Poetry" (Chuncui de shi 纯粹的诗) to discuss the poetics of Moore, in which he mentions that he received a copy of *Confessions of a Young Man* (1888)[1] from the author:

> This year George Moore is seventy-four years old. Three or four months ago he was very ill, but now he's recovered. As soon as he got out of the hospital he sent me a copy of the revised edition of *Confessions of a Young Man* published lately by Traveller's Library. The letter I sent to thank him should have arrived.
>
> George Moore 今年已七十四岁，三四个月前他病得很重，现已全愈，他一出病院便寄给了我一册最近由 Traveller's Library 出版的 Confessions of A Young Man 增订本。我去谢他的信，大概已收到了。[2]

In the same year Shao published a translation of the book's chapter VIII entitled "Letter" (Xin 信), and an article that pivots on Verlaine entitled "A Sort of Cross Between a Thieves' Kitchen and a Presbytery" (Zeiku yu shengmiao zhijian de xintu 贼窟与圣庙之间的信徒), in which he starts with Moore:

> I read Moore's *Confessions of a Young Man*. This is the kind of memoir in my dream [...] I think a life like his is a real life, a life that we need. I've read his *Evelyn Innes*; that's the miniature of his ideal life. Yesterday I

---

[1] It is a memoir about Moore's bohemian life in Paris and London in the 1870s and 1880s. The book is also considered one of the earliest English writings that introduce the French Impressionists.
[2] Shao, *Collected Works of Shao Xunmei*, 189.

bought a copy of his *Memoirs of My Dead Life*; now I come across another part that I like.

我读了马蔼的《一个少年的忏悔录》，啊，这才是我理想中的忏悔录吓 [...] 我以为像他那一种生活，才是真的生活，才是我们所需要的生活。我是读过他的 Evelyn Innes 的，那是他理想生活的缩影。昨天，我又去买了一本他的《我的死了的生活的回忆》，啊，我又读到了一段我所爱读的。³

This part that he likes is Moore's description of his encounter with Verlaine in chapter VII of *Memoirs of My Dead Life* (1906),⁴ from which the title of this article derives.⁵ In 1929 Shao translated "Euphorion in Texas", chapter XII of *Memoirs of My Dead Life*,⁶ and published it first in the inaugural issue of *La Maison D'Or Monthly* and later as an offprint. He writes in the prelude:

"Memory is a middle-aged man's capital", Turgenev says it in his beautiful stories. Our author here is good at tasting and using this capital [...] I'm honored that last summer he presented me with a copy of his *Confessions of a Young Man*; now to print this chapter as an offprint would be a little gift that expresses my appreciation.

'回忆是中年人的资产'， Turgenev 曾在他的美丽的故事中说过。我们的作者便是最善于享受及使用这种资产的 [...] 很荣幸，去年夏天，作者曾赠我他的 Confessions of a Young Man 一册；把这一节印成单行本，也算是感谢他而回敬他的一件小小的礼物。⁷

In the same year, Shao translated Moore's "The Hermit's Love Story" (Heshang de qingshi 和尚的情史), a short story that first appeared in *Cosmopolitan* and *Nash's Magazine* in 1927 and was later added as chapter LVIII in the third American edition of *A Storyteller's Holiday* (1928). Also in this year, he wrote an

---

³ Ibid., 65.
⁴ It is another memoir about Moore's bohemian life in Paris.
⁵ "A sort of cross between a thieves' kitchen and a presbytery. He is the poet Verlaine. The singer of the sweetest verses in the French language—a sort of ambling song like a robin's. You have heard the robin singing on a coral hedge in autumn-tide; the robin confesses his little soul from the topmost twig; his song is but a tracery of his soul, and so is Verlaine's." Moore, *Memoirs of My Dead Life* (New York: D. Appleton and Company, 1914), 81.
⁶ Translated by Shao as "Wode silede shenghuode huiyi 我的死了的生活的回忆".
⁷ Shao, *Collected Works of Shao Xunmei*, 398.

article that concerns Moore's rendering of Longus' *Daphnis and Chloe*,[8] in which he mentions yet another interaction of the two: "Today I received the English translation of *Daphnis and Chloe* published by Heinemann in 1924[9] with George Moore the translator's signature." ("今天收到由伦敦寄来一九二四年 Heinemann 出版的 Daphnis and Chloe 英译限止本，有译者 G. Moore 亲笔签着名。")[10]

The correspondence between the two carried on into 1930 when Shao translated "Priscilla and Emily Lofft"[11] (Zimei 姊妹) and published a long paper entitled "George Moore"[12] that talks about his life and works chronologically. In 1936 he even wrote in an article entitled "My Life and Love" (Wode shenghuo yu lianai 我的生活与恋爱) that "it is completely because of his [Moore's] endowment that I could enjoy the treasure of literature today" ("1936 年他在《六艺》月刊第 1 期《我的生活与恋爱》提到乔治摩尔的赠书写道：'我今天的所以能够享受文学的宝藏，完全是他的赐予'").[13] This is very high praise, which could be certified by Shao Xiaohong's recollection:

> Dad's favorite books were displayed in his bedroom. In the lower part of the cabinet that has doors on both sides are drawers, and the top is a bookshelf. The complete collection of his most adored George Moore (green hardbacks) and the full series of *Yellow Book* (yellow hardbacks) share this space.
>
> 爸爸最珍爱的书则陈列在他卧室里，那口两侧有柜门的大橱当中下部是抽屉，上部则是个书柜。他最尊敬的乔治摩尔的全集 (绿色的精装本) 和全套 Yellow Book (黄色的精装本) 共占此席。[14]

Moore is known more as a prose writer. It is true that his only two poetry collections, *Flowers of Passion* (1878) and *Pagan Poems* (1881), never outsold his prose works such as *Muslin* (1886), *Esther Waters* (1894) and *The Brook Kerith: A Syrian Story* (1916). However, Shao writes in "Pure Poetry" that even

---

[8] Longus is often considered the author of the ancient Greek romance *Daphnis and Chloe*. His life is unknown and it is assumed that he lived on Lesbos in the second century AD.
[9] Moore, *The Pastoral Loves of Daphnis and Chloe* (London: William Heinemann, 1924).
[10] Ibid., 201.
[11] A story included in *In Single Strictness* (London: William Heinemann, 1922).
[12] The original title is in English.
[13] Shao Xiaohong, *My Father Shao Xunmei*, 55.
[14] Ibid., 243.

so "he is simultaneously a poet, an extraordinary poet" ("同时他也是个诗人，一个不同寻常的诗人") and that "he is just like Landor[15] whose light of *Gebir* is shaded by the wide circulation of *Imaginary Conversations*" ("他也如 Landor 一般，因了 Imaginary Conversations 的家诵户传而竟将 Gebir 的光辉给遮掩了").[16] The analogy here is a good one as Moore does like the maneuver of imaginary dialogue, such as those deployed in Landor's *Imaginary Conversations,* and he experiments extensively on writing literary criticism in the form of imaginary dialogue, which is evident in his *Avowals* (1919), *Conversations in Ebury Street* (1924) and the introduction to *Pure Poetry: An Anthology* (1924). These works are the works that Shao cites most when it comes to Moore. In these works, there are jarring dialogues and prose alternating with verse, which ends up in a zone that I would describe as prose poetry.

This idea of prose poetry could be detected from certain works of Shao, such as "Conversations of One Man", a column Shao started in *Human Words Weekly* (Renyan zhoukan 人言周刊) in 1934. Shao writes in the commencement of the series:

> "Conversations of One Man", what a fantastic title! Under this title I can talk to people without being challenged by their questions. I can speak to myself without the sadness of a monologue. I can talk about whatever I want; if I get it wrong, changing it won't be as embarrassing as in a speech. Conversations of one man could have no limits. No one can confine me. These conversations could be fragmentary, could have no continuity. They could even be illogical, for there's only me in this world; if I want freedom, freedom is mine.
>
> 《一个人的谈话》，这是一个多么好的题目！这个题目之下，我可以和人谈话，而不被人家的问句来难住；我可以一个人说话，而不会像独白般的感伤；要谈什么便谈什么，说错了，不见得和演讲一样不好意思更改。一个人谈话，可以完全没有限制，谁也不能给我什么范围。这谈话可以是片段的，可以没有连续性，甚至可以不合逻辑的；因为这一个世界里只有我一个人，我要自由，自由便是我的。[17]

Shao Xiaohong recalls in *My Father Shao Xunmei* that Shen Congwen wrote to Shao after reading "Conversations of One Man": "Xunmei, your 'Conversations

---

[15] Walter Savage Landor (1775-1864) was a British poet and writer. His most notable works are the poem "Gebir" (1798) and the prose *Imaginary Conversations* (1824).
[16] Shao, *Collected Works of Shao Xunmei,* 187.
[17] Shao, *Conversations of One Man,* 6.

of One Man' is the most beautiful prose poem that I've read." ("他读后写信给洵美说：'洵美啊，你的《一个人的谈话》是我所看到的最美的散文诗。'")[18] Here she puts in a note: "Zucheng [Shao's eldest son] asked dad: 'Why did he call it a prose poem?' He replied: 'He means a poem-like prose, a poem in a prose form. George Moore used to write things like that.'" (笔者注: 祖丞曾经问爸爸，'为什么称作散文诗?' 洵美说: '他是指诗一般的散文，散文形式的诗。乔治摩尔写过这样的作品'。)"[19] Judging from this account, it could be deduced that Shao's notion of prose poetry was influenced by Moore.

Though Shen is also frequently judged by critics regarding the music of his works, he is predominantly a prose writer. To him, prose is a conveyer, which entails the dichotomy of form and content, or I can say the conception of a body and its inscription. In Shen's prose works, he often names music directly and writes about musical performances, the education of music and the lack of it, as well as their cultural, socio-historical underpinnings and ramifications. The musical performances, the education of music and the lack of it is treated by him as the content of his prose and also at the same time the form of the cultural, socio-historical underpinnings and ramifications. However much they resemble what was at the time predominantly conceived as prose, Shao still considered his prose poems to be the works of a poetry practitioner. To him, poetry is not a vessel. It does not have, and cannot convey anything other than itself. In Shao's poems, including his prose poems, music is often not easily perceived, as it is to him a condition that cannot be dissected into the dichotomy of content and form and placed in a polemical analysis.

Throughout his career, Shao had only a few short stories published, in contrast with an abundance of poems and critical essays. In 1928 he published his short story debut "Moving Home" (Banjia 搬家), which Yu Dafu 郁达夫[20] describes in a letter to Shao as "having a taste of George Moore, an ethereal story that lately we've rarely seen" ("郁达夫在写给洵美的信里说：'《搬家》大有乔治马蔼的风味，是近来少见的飘逸的文章'").[21] However, despite the applause, Shao admits that writing a "story" is not easy for him. He states:

> So when I lift my pen, and realize a story would have no end, I'm unnerved. I started a novel once. After twenty thousand words, I couldn't

---

[18] Shao Xiaohong, *My Father Shao Xunmei*, 154-155.
[19] Ibid.
[20] Yu Dafu (1896-1945) was a writer and poet. He attended Tokyo Imperial University. His most notable works are the collection of short stories *Sinking* (Chenlun 沉沦) (1921) and a collection of diaries entitled *Nine Kinds of Diaries* (Riji jiuzhong 日记九种) (1927).
[21] Shao Xiaohong, *My Father Shao Xunmei*, 54.

make a girl come downstairs no matter how: she has a lot of reasons to come down, but she has a lot of reasons not to. So I ended up throwing my draft into a drawer, and left her upstairs […] The people in my words would often fight me, disobey my will! I want him to laugh; he's not happy. I want him to cry; he's just not sad. They're so stubborn that my temper erupts; so the world is quiet again.

所以我提起笔来，一想到故事会没有完日，便气馁了。我曾开始过一部小说，写了二万多字，总没有方法叫一位小姐走下楼：她有许多要下楼的理由，但是她也有许多不要下楼的理由，结果我只能把草稿丢进抽屉里，让她一个人留在楼上 […] 我的书中人又时常会对我反抗，违拗我的意志！我要他笑，他偏不快乐；我要他哭，他偏不悲伤。倔强到我发了脾气，世界便又只得静止了。[22]

Note the occurrence of the term "story". Shao states that his difficulty lies in that "a story would have no end" and that he could not wrestle with the organic life of the piece of writing. Shao's notion of prose poetry could not stand alone without his unique concept of the story, which he draws from Moore. Shao retells in *One Man's Conversations* an Irish folklore story, featured in Moore's *A Storyteller's Holiday*, about two talented bards Curithir and Liadin who fall in love with each other. This love causes Curithir to lose his poetic caliber and Liadin to gain a troublesome ability that her songs become sexually arousing to her audience. They are then divided by the church. As Curithir is forced to leave Liadin, Shao narrates the end of the story as follows:

To see Curithir she tried to climb up a tree, but fell into the sea from a rock. When he came back with hair white, Liadin's tomb was covered with trees. So he let go of his soul among the trees. Folks on the island knowing this, buried him beside Liadin's tomb. Soon his tomb was also covered with trees; branches and branches were tangled with those on Liadin's. Trees yielded bright red berries, as red as Liadin's lips.

她因为要爬上树顶去看古立，却从岩石上跌下了海。等古立白了头发回来，丽婷的墓上已长满了山树。他于是从中间把自己的灵魂放走，岛上的居民知道这段故事，便把他葬在丽婷的墓旁。不久他墓上也长满了山树，一根

---

[22] Shao, *Collected Works of Shao Xunmei*, 18.

根的树枝都和丽婷墓上的树枝连了起来，山树结着鲜红的果子，红得和丽婷的嘴唇一样。²³

What was not consummated in the earthly life is here consummating in an earthly garden. The bodies of Curithir and Liadin are decomposed and recomposed into the form of trees. In this piece of prose, life does not take a single form but cycles and recycles in the globe of the story. Though Shao is predominantly a poet, this prose does inspire him when it comes to the decomposition of the body in the unity of "story". When Shao refers to "story", it is not meant as the conventional jargon that one often associates with the content of a piece of prose. He writes:

> Story, is to write-alive everything. To write a tree, it's not enough that it would just wave when wind comes. We need to give it life; instead of moving, it should be living. To write a human, it's not enough that he can move and speak; he needs to breathe and think. Congwen's novels have what I call 'story': the making of a living realm. What Aristotle refers to in Poetics as "the imitation of nature" is to "create a nature the same as the one created by god".

> 故事，即是把一切的东西写得活起来。写棵树，不一定说风来时它会摆动就完事，我们还得给它生命；非但会动，还要会活。写人不一定会动作，会说话就完事，他还得会呼吸，会思想。从文的小说里都有我所说的那种'故事'：一个活的境界的创造。亚理斯多德在《诗学》里所说的"模仿自然"，即是说"创造一个和上帝所创造出来的一样的自然"。²⁴

Here Shao uses the example of Shen Congwen to illustrate his notion of "story": the making of a living realm. As he also cites Aristotle's *Poetics*, it could be deduced that his notion of "story" does not simply apply to Shen's novels, or any piece of prose, but also to poetry, or something primordial that transcends the distinction between prose and verse. This making of a living realm entails the decomposition of the conception of the body and the removal of personality. In this way, the diversity of bodies would traverse to a state of unity, the life of arts.

Like Shao, Moore has a tendency to use words that pertain to music, which is epitomized by a quiz that he gives in *Avowals* asking an imaginary guest to

---

[23] Shao, *Collected Works of Shao Xunmei*, 9-10.
[24] Shao, "Undecayed Stories" (Buxiu de gushi 不朽的故事), *Collective Works of Shao Xunmei*, 140-141.

guess from his verbal description of three pieces of music the composers' names. The three hints are as follows:

> The first piece was a quintet. The instruments employed were clarinet, violins, viola and violoncello, and in the first movement the composer seemed to have thought only of the melody he might give to the clarinet; and a great pour of rich voluptuous song he gave to it on a background of strings vaguely murmuring, twittering dimly, the cello uttering now and then a few grave notes. And my imagination lighting up at the idea half expressed, I said: a nightingale sings in a bare elm branch, keeping the birds in the hedgerow awake; linnets, willow-wren, chaffinch and garden warbler, cannot sleep, so overpowering is the song [...] And then the viola awoke suddenly and my thoughts began to seek some bird to which to match it, but before pitching upon one the clarinet, just like a nightingale, compelled me to give all my thoughts to it [...]
>
> I cannot give as picturesque a description of the second quintet for the same instruments: clarinet, viola, violins and violoncello, for the piece did not evoke any picture or image in my mind, only a certain admiration for the skill with which the composer broidered the clarinet into the musical texture, never leaving it to outsing the other instruments [...]
>
> The third piece, I said, began with fifteen or twenty bars of jiggering rhythm that anybody could write if he chose to transcribe what he might hear in a barn in which peasants had assembled for dancing, a ragged prelude to a second movement, one in which I faintly apprehended a sort of chant intended to represent monks singing in a monastery.[25]

Later he writes that "the point I wish to make is that these three pieces of music tell how art is inspired in the first period, sustained by craft, skill, erudition in the second, and falls afterwards into sterile eccentricities".[26] Interestingly, the three points that he derives from these three pieces correspond with Shao's evolution as a poet. Note that in the description of the first piece there comes an imaginary nightingale, which leads a group of birds: linnets, willow-wren, chaffinch and garden warbler. This bears in idea a striking resemblance to Shao's composition of "Nightingale" and "A Night of Schubert", which I have discussed earlier in the book. That this bird is chosen by Shao as the perfect

---

[25] George Moore, *Avowals* (New York: Boni and Liveright, 1919), 306-307.
[26] Ibid., 308.

symbol for harmony is due to the inspiration of Swinburne, which accords with Moore's summary of "how art is inspired in the first period". The second description mentions the broidering of "musical texture", which again resonates with Shao's rendering of Sitwell's notion of texture. This is in line with Moore's observation that "art is…sustained by craft, skill, erudition" in the second phase. However, Moore gives a rather sarcastic description for the third phase of art as a fall into "sterile eccentricities". What he implies might be that the over-emphasis on craft, skill and erudition will eventually lead to a kind of art that is eccentric and sterile in significance. This could be perceived as a creative stagnation of an artist, which Shao concedes in "Conversations of One Man":

> It was three years ago. In nine months I only wrote two poems […] I know my poems are completely *made*, lacking inspiration. […] My skills have built me a prison.

> 是三年前的事了，九个月中只写了两首诗 […] 我知道我的诗完全是做出来的，缺乏灵感。[…] 我的技巧便为我自己造下了一座囚牢。27

This period of stagnation was not broken until 1936, when Shao published his third poetry collection *Twenty-five Poems*, some eight years after his second collection *Flower-like Evil*. In the preface of *Twenty-five Poems* Shao elaborates on how this "prison" had confined his growth as a poet:

> My poetry journey is odd. From Sappho I found her admirer Swinburne […] At that time I was only looking for voluptuous words, novel phrases and clanging sounds […] Perhaps this is a trial that everyone who writes poetry needs to go through, for we're first moved by poetry often owing to a line or two of shallow philosophy, sweet nothings or a hymn to carnal desire.

> 我的诗的行程也真奇怪，从莎茀发见了她的崇拜者史文朋 […] 当时只求艳丽的字眼，新奇的词句，铿锵的音节 […] 也许这是每一个写诗人所必然地要经受的试探。因为我们第一次被诗来感动，每每是为了一两行浅薄的哲学，或是缠绵的情话，或是肉欲的歌颂。28

The "voluptuous words, novel phrases and clanging sounds" gives an allusion to Shao's earlier works influenced by Swinburne. In the last sentence of the

---

27 Shao, *Collected Works of Shao Xunmei*, 6.
28 Ibid., 368.

excerpt, he writes that this trial for poetry practitioners also includes "a hymn to carnal desire", which can be seen as a self-mockery of his sex-s(t)imulating flower-woman poems written under the influence of Sitwell. Here one can deduce that in the 30s, the influence of Swinburne on Shao was waning, and Shao also found his poetic practices in accordance with Sitwell's notion of texture going into a confinement of eccentricity. The way he broke through the creative stagnation is to assimilate new influence into his poetics, which features predominantly Moore's idea of "pure poetry".

3.1.2 Moore's conception of pure poetry

In July 1928 Shao published an article entitled "D. G. Rossetti", in which "I" and another voice start with a dialogue that talks about celebrating the 100th anniversary of Rossetti's birth, the way of which, metapoetically, is for "me" to write an article that talks about the very subject. As the conversation progresses to the second part of the article, which is named after Rossetti's painting "Beata Beatrix",[29] "I" starts to talk about the resemblance of Dante's loss of Beatrice to Rossetti's loss of Elizabeth Siddal,[30] as well as the assumption that Rossetti models the painted Beatrice after his deceased wife. Here "I" quotes a letter from Moore, which could be seen as an embedded dialogue within a dialogue:

> Four months ago Mr. George Moore replied to me about a letter regarding Rossetti that I sent him ("George Moore 先生在四个月前答我给他一封关于 Rossetti 的信中说"): "I love Rossetti's Mary Magdalene sonnet. It moves me greatly…Once I had the pleasure of showing the picture belonging to that sonnet to a woman friend who had loved that sonnet for 17 years, and had repeated it to herself almost every day for these 6000 and more days. When at last she saw the picture (which was hung very low on the wall, and could not be seen clearly when one was standing), she went down on her knees in the crowded gallery in order to see it properly!"[31]

---

[29] An oil on canvas painting completed in 1870 about Beatrice Portinari (1265-1290), the inspiration for Dante Alighieri's *The New Life* (La Vita Nuova) (1295). She also appears in *Divine Comedy* (La Divina Commedia) (1320) as a guide of Dante. At the end of "Purgatorio", the second part of the poem succeeding "Inferno" and preceding "Paradiso", Beatrice takes over the role of guide from Virgil, as he cannot enter Paradise for being a pagan.

[30] Elizabeth Eleanor Siddall (1829-1862) was a British artist and the wife of Rossetti. She was painted by many Pre-Raphaelite artists including William Holman Hunt and John Everett Millais.

[31] Shao, *Conversations of One Man*, 163.

This sonnet is "Mary Magdalene at the Door of Simon the Pharisee" (1869), which shares the name with the painting (1858). Moore seems to suggest the significance of the poem could also be perceived in the painting. This could be certified by his remark in *An Anthology of Pure Poetry*: "Poetry stands between music and painting, sharing their qualities."[32] In this sense, Moore regards poetry as something that cannot be ontologically detached from music and painting. However, in this anthology, Moore also proposes a notion of "pure poetry". One might wonder what purity denotes when poetry shares qualities with music and painting. Helmut E. Gerber observes:

> Moore wrote no forthright and orderly omnium-gatherum of his artistic opinions and impressions. Everything he wrote was a prolegomenon to the principles which underlay his lifelong endeavor to write pure poetry, whether it took the specific form of verse or of prose, a poetry, which, ideally, he hoped, might aspire to the purity of music.[33]

Here Gerber states that Moore's conception of pure poetry might "aspire to the purity of music". In his conjecture the purity denotes a condition of music, and pure poetry refers to the entity that governs the shared qualities between poetry and music. In another word, this is a condition where the boundary of poetry and music dissolves.

It is true that Moore does not have systematic and well-clarified principles for his notion of pure poetry. The instances where he mentions the term are quite scattered, and whenever it is mentioned, the explanation is short and general, resembling a prolegomenon. Moore's most notable prolegomenon on pure poetry might be a single sentence in *Conversations in Ebury Street*: "Pure poetry is [...] something that the poet creates outside of his own personality."[34] This brief statement about pure poetry and (the exclusion of) "personality" gets extended in his introduction to *An Anthology of Pure Poetry*, which Shao cites in his essay "Pure Poetry":

> It [the phrase of "art for art's sake"] has been babbled for the last thirty or forty years, very few caring to ask themselves if art could be produced for other than aesthetic reasons, and the few that did fall to thinking do

---

[32] George Moore, *An Anthology of Pure Poetry* (New York: Liveright, 1973), 43.
[33] Helmut E. Gerber, "George Moore: From Pure Poetry to Pure Criticism", *The Journal of Aesthetics and Art Criticism* 25, no. 3 (1967): 290.
[34] George Moore, *Conversations in Ebury Street* (London: William Heinemann, 1936), 199.

not seem to have discovered that art for art's sake means pure art, that is to say, a vision almost detached from the personality of the poet.

三四十年来只是喋喋着，很少有去问问他们自己说艺术的产生是否除了唯美的以外还有别的动机，而这些很少个稍加思索的人们也并不见得悟到为艺术而艺术便解作纯粹的艺术，便是说，是一种几乎脱离了诗人的个性的默示。[35]

This babbling might have lasted a bit longer than "thirty or forty years", as Poe in his essay "The Poetic Principle" (published posthumously in 1850) had already engaged with the discussion of the (non)existence of poetry's autotelicity:

> We have taken it into our heads that to write a poem simply for the poem's sake, and to acknowledge such to have been our design, would be to confess ourselves radically wanting in the true poetic dignity and force: – but the simple fact is that would we but permit ourselves to look into our own souls we should immediately there discover that under the sun there neither exists nor can exist any work more thoroughly dignified, more supremely noble, than this very poem, this poem per se, this poem which is a poem and nothing more, this poem written solely for the poem's sake.[36]

Here Poe points out that the attempt to write a poem for the poem's sake has often been equated with the reluctant admittance of our poetry lacking "true poetic dignity and force". However, he then argues that there is no causality between the assumed lack and the attempt—writing a poem for its own sake is not a consequent action to try to fix this assumably preceding lack—and that what is assumably lacking does not actually lack in a poem that is written for its own sake. Poe maintains that a poem written for its own sake is always-already "thoroughly dignified" and "supremely noble". Note that these attributes are usually associated with human beings. By using these phrases, he is describing this poem as a human body, and this body would be inevitably

---

[35] Moore, *An Anthology of Pure Poetry*, 19; Shao's translation is in "Pure Poetry", *Collected Works of Shao Xunmei*, 187.
[36] Here quoted from Edgar Allan Poe, *The Works of Edgar Allan Poe, Vol 3* (London: A&C Black, 1899), 202.

inscribed. The inscription might be what Moore calls personality. Let us look at a later (but earlier than Moore) interpretation of pure poetry by A. C. Bradley:[37]

> Pure poetry is not the decoration of a preconceived and clearly defined matter [...] If the poet already knew exactly what he meant to say, why should he write the poem? [...] It was not a fully formed soul asking for a body: it was an inchoate soul in the inchoate body of perhaps two or three vague ideas and a few scattered phrases. The growing of this body into its full stature and perfect shape was the same thing as the gradual self-definition of the meaning [...] if we insist on asking for the meaning of such a poem, we can only be answered "It means itself."[38]

The "two or three vague ideas" and "a few scattered phrases" would be the initial, inchoate inscription of this inchoate body. The equation of "the growing of this body into its full stature and perfect shape" with "the gradual self-definition of the meaning" adopts the same maneuver of Poe's as it compares a poem to a human body and uses the organic integrity of human body to illuminate the autotelicity of "a poem written for its own sake".

If I return to Moore's conception of pure poetry, the difference or development from that of Poe and Bradley would be that he abandons the dialectic of the human body in the conception of pure poetry. The abandonment does not mean that Moore negates Poe and Bradley's notion that the poem has a humanoid body. What Moore proposes is that the body of the poet is different from the body of the poem, which has its own life independent of the poet's. In the statement that pure poetry is "something that the poet creates outside of his own personality", personality is Moore's rendering of the concept of a single inscribed body. "Outside of" denotes the removal of the conception of the body, the underpinning for the dichotomy of "I" and "other". When the body is removed and the dichotomy of "I" and "other" collapses, there will not be an "other's" sake but the unitary sake of the poem.

If one brings back Gerber's conjecture that pure poetry refers to a condition where the boundary between poetry and music dissolves, one could see that Moore's notion of pure poetry as the removal of the conception of the body might be seen as a preliminary instruction to reach this condition. This is because Gerber is a poetic critic, an observer, while Moore is a practitioner of poetry. However, Moore does not put this idea into practice as he did not

---

[37] Andrew Cecil Bradley (1851-1935) was a British literary critic. His most notable works include *Shakespearean Tragedy* (1904) and *Oxford Lectures on Poetry* (1909).
[38] A. C. Bradley, "Poetry for Poetry's Sake: An Inaugural Lecture Delivered on June 5, 1901", *Oxford Lectures on Poetry* (New Delhi: New Delhi Atlantic Publishers & Dist, 1999), 23.

publish any poetry in his later life. He died in 1933, nine years after he put forth interesting prolegomena to the notion of "pure poetry" in *Conversations in Ebury Street* and *An Anthology of Pure Poetry*.

That being said, this preliminary instruction was taken by Shao through the migration of influence. The removal of the conception of the body provides for Shao a possible breakthrough from his creative stagnation and a reconsideration of his previous treatment of woman's body in poetry. To Shao, the conception of the body always denotes in a poem a cohesive, unitary poetic voice. And his approach to the removal of the conception of the body is to replace the dialectic of the body with the dialogic of voices, which I will discuss in the next section.

3.2 The dialogic of pure poetry

3.2.1 Prose poetry and the use of dialogic

In section 3.1.1 I have mentioned that Shao gets the idea of prose poetry from Moore, as the later Moore frequently engages with a kind of writing that effaces the boundary between prose and verse. To Shao, this also represents a possible means to remove the conception of the body. His experiments in prose poetry could be epitomized by "Josephine", which unfolds with the following lines:

> The village in which I live is called Bourg-la-Reine, don't know how many minutes of train it takes to reach Robinson forest.
> Go to Robinson.
> Rather than saying the landlord's daughter Josephine likes to hang out with me, I'd say it's my asking too sincerely that makes her agree. That's where French women are lovely.
> Josephine is a petite countrygirl.
> Josephine's hair is light yellow.
> Josephine's face is like a cat——her temper too.
> Josephine's eyes are like cat eyes.
> Josephine's teeth are a row of orderly diamonds——just not quite white.
> Josephine's voice is sometimes too thin, people say.
> Josephine can sing——sings often, if not with words then hums tunes.

> 我住的那个小村落叫做 Bourg-la-Reine，不晓得坐多少分钟的火车便可以到 Robinson 树林。
> 到 Robinson 去。
> 假使说房东的女儿 Josephine 喜欢和我作伴，不如说是我要求得太恳切了，她不得不答应。法国女人的可爱便在这里。

Josephine 是个小小身材的村女。
Josephine 的头发是淡黄的。
Josephine 的屑儿像只猫——脾气也像只猫。
Josephine 的眼睛也像猫眼睛。
Josephine 的牙齿是一排齐的小方块——就只不大白。
Josephine 说话的声音有时太细了，别人这样讲。
Josephine 会唱——时常唱，不唱字句便哼着调子。 39

It seems at the very beginning that Josephine is subject to a fervid gaze from "I", the male beholder. The enumeration of her body parts—hair, face, eyes, teeth—seems like a maneuver similar to the treatment of other female bodies that occur in Shao's poems. However, as the text progresses, the body of Josephine seems to disappear:

> Off the train, went uphill. Josephine comes here often, now a guide. The sky was a bit gray, we were not afraid of rain. I said we should've brought an umbrella, she said I'm too unromantic. Are there any Chinese poets? Turning right can't be wrong. She said it'd be closer.
> We were among thorns, she walked, picked and ate berrylike stuff. Asked me to pick and eat. Gave me one to try.
> My pants were pierced by the thorns, her clothes got some holes, so happy she went Oh! Oh! Oh!
> Found a thornless clearing, seems that there are people often; sugar boxes, cigarette butts, hundreds-wrinkled handkerchiefs……
> Josephine said she's tired, wants to lie down. I took off my coat, laid it on the ground. She said no mattress needed, better curl it to a pillow.
> Josephine does not believe there're fairies in the forest.
> She asked if the hair of Chinese women's all black. She loves black hair, especially men with black hair.
> I can't think of a word.
> Six o'clock.
> Too cold, squeezed together and walked.
> Josephine said a glass of cognac'd be good for us.

> 下了火车，登坡。Josephine 是常来的，做领队。天有些灰暗，我们都不怕下雨。我说我们应当带顶伞来，她说我太不 Romantic 了。中国人有没有诗人？

---

39 Shao Xunmei, *Guizuqu* 贵族区 [The Aristocrats' Neighborhood] (Shanghai: Shanghai shudian chubanshe, 2012), 97-98.

向右手转弯是不会错的。她说这样走比较近。

我们在荆棘中间,她一壁走一壁采着桑子般的东西吃。也叫我采了吃。先给我一颗尝尝。

我的裤子被荆棘刺破了,她的衣裳有了几个小洞,她快乐得 Oh! Oh! Oh!

找到一处没有荆棘的空地,看来时常有人来; 糖匣子, 香烟屁股, 百绉的小手帕……

Josephine 说累了,要躺一忽。我把外衣脱了铺在地上。她说用不到褥子,卷起来做枕头好。

Josephine 不相信树林里有仙人。

她问我中国女人的头发是不是都是黑的。她爱黑头发,尤其是黑头发的男子。

我想不出话来。

六点钟。

冷得紧,挤在一块走。

Josephine 说喝杯 Cognac 对于我们一定好。[40]

It should be noted that here Josephine is another poetic voice. The previous enumeration of her body parts only exists in the descriptive account of "I". Instead of being instrumentalized as a means to achieve a sexual and musical consummation, Josephine has a vocal capacity that the female bodies quoted in the previous chapter do not possess. She has her own voice instead of being simply a receiver of a unitary poetic voice, the male "I". Her making of music does not rely on the plucking of a unitary "I"; her agency is intact in her singing. The voices of Josephine and "I" engage in a dialogue and the conception of a sole narrator or a definite poetic voice is effaced in this dialogic exchange. The biunivocal takes over the monotonic; what dwells in the text is no longer a female body ardently gazed at, but two voices that talk to each other.

If "Josephine" seems to be a prose poem nearer to the end of prose when measured on the pole of homogeneity, one could also examine Shao's prose poems that seem to lean towards what is conventionally regarded as verse. A great example is "Voice" (Shengyin 声音), which begins as follows:

> Summer night amid the thunder rain, there's
> A strange voice saying to me, I've gone wrong
> On the way I go, in the cloud no rainbow can be found,
> Among willow leaves there's no guarantee of
> Peach blossoms' shadow.

---

[40] Ibid., 98.

> This morning, an angel unknown
> dropped an ordinary letter, from the door crack:
> The charming font symbolizes a vague
> News, she gave me happiness, than happiness she gave me
> More scary hazards.
>
> 夏夜在雷雨的中间,有一个
> 陌生的声音对我说,我已走错了
> 我要走的路,在白云里不能去找虹,
> 在杨柳的绿叶里也不一定有
> 桃花的影子。
> 今早,不知名的天使
> 投进一封平常的信,从门缝里:
> 迷醉的字体象征一个含糊的
> 新闻,她给我幸福,她给我比幸福
> 更可怕的灾害。[41]

In the first stanza, "a strange voice" is designated before "I" appears. This voice other than "me" starts the dialogue and points out that trying to find rainbows in clouds and peach blossoms in willow trees is a wrong way to go. This is a voice that denies poesis' ability to create and become. As the text reaches the second stanza, a letter delivered by an angel cues the existence of another voice, the voice of "she". What does she say in the letter?

> I don't want to be a lamp moth, nor willing
> With my fire to burn the inextinguishable fire,
> I know hungry eyes would find their intoxicating
> Food ——so even God has moments when he can't tell
> The reason: when he's to forbid flying
> With wings, love with feelings, singing with desire
> Songs that he himself has never prepared.
>
> But a poem cannot stop like this,
> Just as God has his inexhaustible stories.
> She wants me to reply, (I can't think of words against my will)
> I say I like happiness and fear hazards,
> Anyway philosophy is not a virgin's hope,
> White hair's horror can't be the crimson of cherries,

---

[41] Shao, *Poetic Works of Shao Xunmei*, 136.

She wants me to utter the phrase that I forgot,
She wants me to believe a tender flower will
Without season's bullying wither herself;

我不愿做灯蛾，更不愿
把自己的火去烧扑不灭的火，
我知道饥饿的眼睛会找到荼毒的
食粮，——原来上帝也有说不出
理由的时候:当他要禁止有翅膀的
飞，有情感的爱，有痴望的唱出
他自己都不曾预备着的歌声。

但是诗不能就这样地结束，
正如上帝也有他讲不完的故事。
她要我答复，(我想不出违心的话)
我说我喜欢幸福怕灾害，
究竟哲学不是处女的期望，
白发的恐怖不比樱桃的艳红，
她要我讲出我遗忘了的成语，
她要我相信一朵嫩弱的花不用
季候的欺侮她自己会凋零;[42]

The gathering of a lamp moth and fire denotes that this is presumably a letter that enunciates an intention to reject a one-directional love. But the poem does not end with the delivery of this voice. "She wants me to reply." This letter, as an embodiment of dialogue, requests a symmetrical, reciprocal action from "my" voice. "The phrase that I forgot" could be deduced as an acceptance of the loss of love, while a tender flower's self withering seems to certify this loss. So what is "my" reply to her voice?

But I fear, I fear compassion would poke through
My solemnity's hypocrisy, a tortured
Innocence. I put my right palm to my left palm,
A monotonous voice makes my reply.
Now I say, if there's alcohol, it'd
Make me give an unexpected acknowledgement:
It might just be a learnt poem,

---

[42] Ibid., 136-137.

Shao, Moore and the idea of pure poetry

A learnt word, a learnt painting;
But they'd all like arrows aim at
The mark, with one shot shoot at the most centered dot.
Now only Jesus would tell you, all
Comfort, reward and charity are on that nail.
Things get big, tears'd be like rain,
Feelings'd be like wind, self has no proposition.
You'll for the first time see soul and body
Each say words they each dare not say.

但是，我怕，我怕让同情揭穿了
我庄严的虚伪，一个摧残了的
天真。我把右手心贴着左手心，
一种单调的声音做了我的回答。
这时候，我说，要是有酒，酒会
使我交出一篇料不到的供状：
虽也许只是一首背熟的诗，
一个想熟的字，一张看熟的画；
可是他们都会像箭头瞄准了
箭靶，一射就射中最里面的一点。
这时候，只有耶稣会对你说，一切的
安慰，报酬和爱都在那一支钉上。
事情就会闹大，眼泪像像雨，
情感会像风，自己会没有主张。
你便会第一次见到灵魂和肉体
各自说出各自不敢说的话。⁴³

Note the sentence "Now only Jesus would tell you". As "my" voice replies to hers, an ambiguous "you" is designated here. It could be a general "you" that refers to the reader, if one assumes that "I" abruptly turn and address us from the stage. What seems more likely would be that as "I" start to reply to "her", "she" is now substituted by "you" in the context of a second-person dialogue. Interestingly, this reply gradually evolves into a hysterical accusation:

Ah I hate there's you in the world, without you
The beating of feelings would have a certain measure.
[…]

---

⁴³ Ibid., 137-138.

I hate you, because you came to me
Like alcohol splashed on a clean table: though I dare not
Start a fire to make red, green or yellow flowers,
But you didn't wait for that crazy moment,
Left on my heart a mark and left.
This mark is made deep as if with whichever
God's power it made the thinnest gold needle
Engraved in an unwashable and unwearable
Place. I don't believe there'd be a second god
That could wipe out this pure mark!

啊，我恨这世上有你，没有你
情感的跳动就有了一定的分寸。
[…]
我恨你，因为你像酒精泼上光净的
桌子般来到我这里:我虽然不敢
燃上火，造出红的，绿的或是黄的花，
但是你却不等那疯癫的时刻到来，
竟在我心上留了片印子走了。
这印子留得深，像是用了不知
那一个神的力，把最细的金针
镌在不能洗涤也不能磨灭的
地方。我不信还会有第二个神
能为我抹去这一个纯洁的痕迹![44]

The hearing of the voice/ the coming of "she" is here compared to an act of alcohol splashing on a clean table. The outcome of this act is leaving a stain on the table, and also metaphorically leaving a mark on "my" heart. This mark is then associated with an act of engraving with "the thinnest gold needle", which illustrates the depth and degree of pain from the refusal of love. The accusation goes on:

> I hate that you don't come to me and say all my
> Impression of you is my own illusion:
> You've never been to my heart, let alone
> Sprinkled in my heart a flowerable
> Seed. I hate why you don't tell me,
> I should've forgotten you like I forget

---

[44] Ibid., 138-139.

Myself when twilight looks as beautiful as dawn.
Lucky that I know what the moon says, she says:
I've never smiled to you, that's the breeze
Flipping my veil, I've never
Shed a tear for you, that's the dewdrop in the cold fog.
I've also never looked at you, my
Light is for everyone's eyes.

我恨你不走来对我说，我所有的
你的印象原是我自己的幻想：
你从没有到过我心里，更没有
在我心里撒过一粒会开花的
种子。我恨你为什么不对我说，
我应当把你忘掉，像我忘掉
我自己，当黄昏长得像早晨般美丽。
啊，幸亏月亮的话我懂得，她说：
我从没有对你笑，那是小凤
带动了我的面纱，我也从没有
对你下泪，那是冷雾里的水花。
我也从没有看过你一次，我的
光明是为了天下人的眼睛。[45]

Here in a dramatic twist "I" claim that "my" impression of "you" could have been but illusionary: "her" voice has never come to "my" heart, and hence no mark is ever left there. "I should've forgotten you like I forget myself." The forgetting of deictics would be a loss of difference. But the proposed forgetting of deictics only exists in a state of absence: "I should've forgotten you like I forget myself" is something that "you don't tell me". So in a world where "you" and "myself" are not forgotten, there is still a difference among voices. A "she" again picks up the microphone and takes over the dominant deictic of "I". What "she" says could be understood as an act of retelling the letter's content in "her" way, in symmetry with the previous accusation made by the male voice. Hence it could be interpreted as a defense made by the female voice:

Don't blame me for letting you down, I've never
Needed your care, pity or service.
You needn't blame me for treating you coldly, for I've

---

[45] Ibid., 139-140.

Never prepared a fervid response.
The fire's yours, the craziness is yours, the gentleness is
Yours, then the sorrow's for you to take.
You don't need to wait for me, my coming and going
Has my own timing: cockcrows
Would prompt me to bed, nightbirds singing
Would cue me to dress, don't you ever think
My daily returns are just for you.

你不用怪我辜负你，我从没有
需要你的爱护，怜惜和侍候。
你也不用怪我冷淡你，因为我
从没有预备着热烈的酬应。
火是你的，痴是你的，温柔是
你的，那懊恼就得由你收受。
你更不用等着我，我的来去
有我自己的时候:雄鸡的啼号
会催我睡眠，晚上小鸟的歌唱
又会催我梳装，你千万不用想
我的朝暮的来去又是为了你。[46]

The voice of "she" states that the accusation of "letting you down" could never stand, for this love is only assumed by the male voice and has never been given "a fervid response" from the female voice. She ends her defense as follows:

That poor man who has seen a deity, he always wants
Himself to go up the firmament. He knows the wax wings
Would melt in the heat of sunshine, he knows
The wind beside the clouds has broken billions of
Iron plumage: but he can never control
The exaltation of desire, like an aerolite
Going towards a planet, he's going towards
You——if you were in a dream and heard
A distant voice were calling your
Name, hearken, it'd be him drawing near!

可怜一个见过仙人的，他总想
自己上天。他明知道蜜腊的羽翼

---

[46] Ibid., 140.

会化尽在火炽的日光里，他明知道
云边的大风曾吹断过几千万对
钢铁的翅膀:但是他总制不住
欲望的超升，像是一颗陨石
要趋向另一个星球，他要趋向
你。——假使你在梦中，听得有
一个遥远的声音在唤着你的
名字，留心，这便是他在走近![47]

Here the voice of "she" relates an Icarus-like story without making "him" a definite Icarus. "The exaltation of desire" drives "him" towards "you". "She" warns the male voice of the possibility of "he" becoming "you" in a hypothesis that "you" get any closer to "me". In this collision of metaphors, she implies that any attempt to get close to "her" will end up in a tragedy. And this vague, hazardous merging of "you" and "he" is the female voice's symmetrical response to the male voice's previous attempt to conglomerate "you" and "she".

Susan Suleiman writes that contemporary feminism should attempt to "get beyond, not only the number one—the number that determines unity of body or of self—but also to get beyond the number two, which determines difference, antagonism and exchange".[48] "The Voice" as the epitome of Shao's use of dialogic in poetry, is in its effect very close to what Suleiman calls "beyond the number two". Here is how Bordo comments on Suleiman's numbers:

> The "number one" clearly represents for Suleiman the fictions of unity, stability, and identity characteristic of the phallocentric worldview. The "number two" represents the grid of gender, which feminists have used to expose the hierarchical, oppositional structure of that worldview. "Beyond the number two" is, not some other number, but "endless complication" and a "dizzying accumulation of narratives." Suleiman here refers to Derrida's often quoted interview with Christie McDonald, in which he speaks of "a 'dream' of the innumerable, . . . a desire to escape the combinatory to invent incalculable choreographies."[49]

---

[47] Ibid., 140-141.
[48] Susan Suleiman, *The Female Body in Western Culture: Contemporary Perspectives* (London: Harvard University Press, 1985), 24.
[49] Susan Bordo, *Unbearable Weight: Feminism, Western Culture, and the Body* (Berkeley: University of California Press, 1993), 226.

One can feel the "endless complication" and "dizzying accumulation of narratives" in the above examination of "The Voice". The poem ends with an atmospheric wrestling of voices, with aerolites flying betwixt and between. The voice of "I" attempts to merge other voices and form a unity, but the diversified voices resist against being conglomerated into a univocal poetic voice. This wrestle is an act of traversing between unity and diversity, where no body is fixed. Through the use of dialogic Shao removes the unitary vocal body of "I" and turns the poem into a dialogue where no closure is assumed.

3.2.2 Pure poetry as the unity of arts

In the previously cited excerpt, one could hear diversified, colliding voices in an atmospheric setting. This almost astrophysical reverie of Shao gravitates towards a piece of writing in Moore's *Conversations in Ebury Street*:

> Everything that has been must of necessity return, return being the law over all things, great and small, stars and mallows alike, everything returning to unity, to spread out again through space and time and again to be collected into unity; and that for ever and ever. A wonderful dream was Poe's, that there is no death and that we are only separated from ourselves by some billions of years.[50]

The act of "everything that has been" returning to unity could be deemed as the end of each and every individual, diversified life, which could be equated with a temporary death. The spreading out of unity "through space and time" designates the diversification of unity, which could be termed as an ephemeral birth. Stars and an all-englobing universe, mallows and the totality of life are two sets "alike", of parallel, homogeneous metaphors that orbit this traversing of diversity and unity. Here Moore suggests that death is but "some billions of years" that separate "ourselves" from "we". Body, and the deictic symbols of body—pronouns and reflexive pronouns—are conglomerated with cosmology. The end of each and every individual "self" in the collective unit of "ourselves" will be the annihilation of the plurality of "ourselves" and hence a step towards retrieving a long lost state of monism that is "some billions of years" away—the singularity of "we", the origin of the universe. "Ourselves" are rendered the embodiment of diversity while "we" are that of unity.

This illustration of unity and diversity resonates with Shao's idea of how a poem comes to be in *Conversations of One Man*:

---

[50] George Moore, *Conversations in Ebury Street*, 8.

> It comes like clouds in the sky: sometimes they're a pure white crystal, static, allowing you to gaze yearningly; sometimes they're a herd of trivial dust, you need to catch them fast, in one second they'll change into hundreds of images; sometimes they're a layer of transparent screen, rippling gently in your soul; sometimes they're a large pile of duskiness, clipping wind, clipping rain. You dare not raise your head and look, but in your heart trembles their majesty.

> 它的来像是天上的云: 有时是一块洁白的结晶，不动，准许你神往地伫视; 有时是一群琐碎的粉片，你要捉得快，一秒钟它会变幻几十百种形象，有时是一层透明的薄翳，在你灵魂里轻微地荡漾; 有时是一大堆的昏暗，夹着风，又夹着雨，你不敢抬头望，但是你心底里震动着它的威严。[51]

The clouds could be "a herd" (yiqun 一群) of trivial dust, "a layer" (yiceng 一层) of transparent screen or "a large pile" (yidadui 一大堆) of duskiness. "In one second they'll change into hundreds of images." They are ever-changing, capable of metamorphosing into various forms. And note the measure words here: "a herd", "a layer" and "a large pile". The plural, collective unit of clouds could become "a" singular entity, being this or that. In this sense, the clouds are also embodying the traversing of diversity and unity. It might seem at first that Shao's idea of unity is atomistic, but the act of never-ending traversing denotes a cyclical process of diversity returning to unity and unity dispersing into diversity, which bears a resemblance to the statement "everything returning to unity, to spread out again" in Moore's astrophysical fantasy from the earlier-discussed excerpt of *Conversations in Ebury Street*.

Now if one combines Moore's proposal of the removal of the conception of the body as the means to reach pure poetry, one could deduce that both Moore and Shao believe that the conception of the body is an embodiment of diversity while pure poetry denotes an ideal, primordial condition of unity. This condition of unity concerns not just the divisions of prose and verse, but also arts of all forms, as the idea of form cannot do without the conception of the body and every art form is but a body that distinguishes it from other bodies. When all the bodies of the different art forms disappear, arts become one. Music and poetry would be united in the condition of pure poetry. This idea is evident in Shao's "Undisputed Faith", where a meta-poem examines itself:[52]

---

[51] Shao, *Conversations of One Man*, 13.
[52] The original title is in English.

Don't suspect me too much, my friend.
Frankly I'd decorate this façade,
But I have too many masterpieces
That'd make the master marvel in the mirror frame
At often unforeseeable changes.
I never plan to hide or boast,
But I know in the changing season's
Air, colors need to have anytime
A new deployment: like on the mountain and tree tops
Spring can't linger on winter's clothes;
Like white snow, it doesn't have a fixed
Form, but it is free in a
Biggest scope [...]

不要过分地怀疑我，朋友。
诚心地我要装饰这墙壁，
但是我有太多的名作
会使主人惊异这镜框里
时常有不可预言的变换。
我并没有想要遮隐或炫耀，
但是我明白在季候更替的
空气里，色调要随时有
新的配置：像是山头和树顶
春天不能留恋冬天的衣裳；
像是白雪，它没有固定的
形式，但是它自由在一个
最大的范围里 [...][53]

The poem is from the very beginning aware of its being as a poem. "The master" here might refer to the poet, someone who thinks that he could master the poem and that his authorship would be definite and self-evident. "The mirror frame" could be the poet's attempt to frame the poem with a certain body. But in the attempt, there emerges "unforeseeable changes" that the poet cannot predict or control. The agency of the poem is here at work. The poem knows well that spring or winter, or any other seasons could be simulated through its play of words. And here white snow, like clouds that I have discussed earlier, is embodying the poem's capability of metamorphosis. The poem goes on:

---

[53] Shao, *Poetic Works of Shao Xunmei*, 146.

I often put in tempting
Paintings that excite the master exceedingly,
And make him think the cosmos
Lost virginity in his bedroom; he has long forgotten
Outside the window curtain that iron face——
Sadly it won't abandon its historical
Esteem. And I often put in
Plain sketches, because what's running
Also faster than time is,
The ephemeral joy, this, you must
Taste in the silence.

我时常会放进诱惑的
图画，使主人过度地兴奋，
使他以为宇宙在他的
卧室里失了节；他早忘却
窗帏外那只铁板的面孔——
可怜它不愿放弃它历史的
尊严。我又时常会放进
平淡的速写，因为跑得
比时光更快的，还有，
刹那间的欢乐，这个，你须在
冷寂中去回味。[54]

Here "tempting paintings" might designate those verbal, well-decorated poems that could easily excite and arouse senses. This might be a sarcasm of Shao's voluptuous works in his early career, where everything is treated with an animating sensuality that makes one think the cosmos might have "lost its virginity", which cues Shao's eccentric rendering of flower-woman that I have discussed in the second chapter. "Plain sketches" on the other hand, denote those that have few adornments but at the same time appear to be way too minimalist, of which Shao has also written a lot. But what kind of poetry does this poem applaud the most?

> […] Also I would often
> Put in some purest works,
> With no designations nor names,
> Just lines and colorful architecture,

---

[54] Ibid., 147.

The architecture might have meaning, but
The creator has never been concerned with its
Result being a failure or success.
It's the trial of truth, you could
With names mold as many illusions.
My friend, my effort might
Make you feel troubled and redundant,
But this is all that I could do:
Try to comfort nature with the artificial.

[…] 我又时常会
放进一些最纯粹的作品,
没有指定也没有名目,
只是线条和色彩的建筑,
这建筑也许有意义, 但是
创造者从没有顾虑到它的
结果是失败或是成功。
这是真理的试探, 你可以
借名来捏造出多少幻象。
朋友, 我的苦心, 也许会
使你感到麻烦和多余,
但这是我所能做的一切:
尽量地把人工去安慰天然。 [55]

"Some purest works" might designate those that are written with an attempt to approach the condition of pure poetry. "You could with names mold as many illusions" is again a meta-poetic statement that bears the same significance with the frequently-casted clouds, which I have discussed earlier. Each name produces an illusion of body/personality/individuality, but the bodies/personalities/individualities that are labelled with the names all come from and will eventually return to a unifying state of monism.

In this chapter, one can see that Shao's attitude towards women goes through a tremendous change in the poems which assimilate the influence of Moore. The woman, who is once treated by Shao merely as an instrument and whose body is grounded in his poems during the period when he was deeply influenced by Sitwell, is now in the post-Moore stage disappearing into the atmosphere, becoming a voice with no body, a voice that is not "the other" voice,

---

[55] Ibid., 147-148.

but a voice among various voices in dialogue. Note that among the "purest works" there is no trace of the word "music", or any words that pertain to music. Music seems to disappear with the woman, the previous instrument Shao manipulates to produce the condition of music in poetry. In general, words associated with music appear much less in Shao's works during this period, which forms a sharp contrast to his early works that abound with musical allusions. In his conception, the poems that become pure poetry are concurrently music, in the unifying monism of pure poetry. The body of music that divides music and poetry disappears, just as the body of woman that divides the woman and "I" dissolves, and music becomes the universal reality of pure poetry, allusions of which thus do not need to be in the poem.

Shao seems to concede that pure poetry, the unity of arts, is an ideal and primordial condition that could never be reached, but simulated with as much effort as possible. A poem or a piece of music could aspire to the condition of pure poetry, but this aspiration could never be completely fulfilled. Poetry or music could only be as close to pure poetry as possible, but yet they could never be ontologically pure poetry. As the obstacle is always-already insuperable, the strategy that Shao puts forth is play. As shown in "Undisputed Faith", writing the "purest works" with his utmost effort is a play of the traversing between unity and diversity, a play of the dialogic process of poetry and music wanting to become one.

Conclusion

Regarding the result of the 2016 US presidential election, Bordo writes in *The Destruction of Hillary Clinton*:

> Since the election, the word "misogyny" has re-entered the cultural bloodstream [...] Clinton Derangement Syndrome, like Obama Derangement Syndrome, is not the result of anything as simple as hatred of women or hatred of blacks. More specifically, it is fueled by anger at those women and blacks who refuse to behave according to the expectations of a culture that hasn't yet processed the deeper recesses of its racism and sexism, a culture that can go through the motions (elect a black president, nominate a woman candidate), but still requires a certain amount of deference—obedience—to The Man.[1]

Bordo finds the result disappointing. The disappointment does not only lie in the fact that Hillary Clinton did not make it to the presidency, but in the "the deeper recesses" of sexism which are saturated with the idea of The Man. Twenty years ago she wrote in "The Feminist as Other" that the most important struggle for feminists "is not over inclusion (the liberal measure of female 'power')", not just about paying more attention to "hiring women and minorities", "but over the cultural meaning of that inclusion."[2] She states that "feminist theory swims up-stream against powerful currents whenever it threatens to assume the mantle of general cultural critique rather than simply advocate for the greater inclusion or representation of women and their 'differences.'"[3] One possible strategy of resistance to these "powerful currents" and The Man whose underpinnings are deeply rooted in the ideas of Descartes, the Enlightenment thinkers as well as the male postmodernists whom he deeply influenced, is for Bordo to resist "the ghettoization of feminist insight", "at conferences, in anthologies, in the curriculum", in PhD research projects I will add, "and insist that feminist philosophy be read as cultural critique. More precisely, we need to insist that 'gender theory' be read for the cultural critique that is implicated in it."[4]

---

[1] Susan Bordo, *The Destruction of Hillary Clinton* (London: Melville House, 2017), 185.
[2] Susan Bordo, "The Feminist as Other", *Metaphilosophy* 1996, vol. 27, no. 1-2: 24.
[3] Ibid., 23.
[4] Ibid.

This book is an attempt to resist "the ghettoization of feminist insight" and bring the feminist skepticism to word and music studies, which by its interdisciplinary nature is itself questioning the cartesian framing of disciplines, subjects and genres, by not just scrutinizing the representations of women playing and writing music, having a musical education or career in literature, but investigating the conception of the woman and her body in possible ideas of the condition of music in poetry. The feminist skepticism also contributes to the study of early twentieth-century Chinese poetry, which is saturated with the idea of The Man through the cultural influence of the West, by examining Shao's poetry and three Anglophone influences in particular. Last but not least, this book brings feminist skepticism to the scholarship of Shao, a male poet born, raised and having lived in colonial Shanghai. Lynn S. Chancer writes in her review of Bordo's *The Male Body: A New Look at Men in Public and in Private*: "Men also stand to benefit from feminism; that feminist scholarship and activism increasingly include men as objects of research and as subjects of change is a sign of progress."[5] The scholarship of Shao can benefit from feminist skepticism, for not only the women, but also the men in China need an emancipation from the idea of "The Man", which saturates the conceptions of gender, race and nationality.

Shao Xunmei was influenced by many authors. When it comes to his idea of the condition of music in poetry, he was most influenced by A. C. Swinburne, Edith Sitwell and George Moore. This book certifies the existence of similarities between Shao and these three authors.

Though the book singles out these three individual writers that influenced Shao when it comes to the condition of music in poetry, the three influences are relevant to each other. Shao came to know the works of Swinburne first, and then those of Sitwell and Moore. But it does not mean that the influences of the three authors take place strictly in a chronological order. Their impact on Shao is often combined and synthesized. Every time Shao gets to know the works of a new author, the significance that he perceives is contrasted with the significance that he has already perceived and assimilated from all the relevant works that he has read. The result of the contrast, or what Shao terms as "the new order", is often a synthesis of the influence assimilated from the new works and the existing ideas of Shao that have been shaped by the previous influences. This means the eventual synthesized influence of a new source on Shao is not solely determined by Shao's reception of the source, but by the inter-reactions of Shao's reception of the new source and his already-synthesized reception of

---

[5] Lynn S. Chancer, "No More Martians?" *The Women's Review of Books* 2000, vol. 17, no. 7: 19.

all the already-inter-reacting sources with which Shao has come into contact prior to the temporal coordinate of Shao's contact with the new source. Shao's idea of the condition of music in poetry is shaped and constantly reshaped in this process.

Swinburne and Shao had no personal contact as the former died three years after Shao was born. However, Shao's biographies confirm that Swinburne is Shao's poetic idol that led him into the career of a poet. Shao's own works also suggest that he was influenced by Swinburne.

This influence takes form in the conception of harmony, a condition where poetry is musical. Swinburne is the one who comes up with the notions of harmony as well as inner and outer music. These terms are not clearly defined in his works, but are frequently deployed in his poetic criticism. Judging from his criticism on Wordsworth, Shelley and Blake, Swinburne's notions of inner and outer music correspond with the meaning and sound of a poem respectively. Harmony, in his conception, denotes the merging of inner and outer music, namely the union of meaning and sound. He considers nature as the perfect paradigm for harmony, which is also evident in Shao's works.

Both Swinburne and Shao see the nightingale as the ideal symbol for harmony. The similarity is certified by their works examined in juxtaposition. Sappho represents to Shao and Swinburne the possibility of poetry. Shao was obsessed with Sappho in his youth, and it is because of this obsession that he came into contact with Swinburne's works. Swinburne was also mesmerized by Sappho in his youth. The two poets consider Sappho as a muse and a great poet to look up to. Sappho's fragments denote that there could be uncountable possibilities about her life and art, and this fragmentation makes Shao and Swinburne see her as the incarnation of poetry and what poetry could be. Both Shao and Swinburne like to merge Sappho and nightingale in their poetic practices. The merging of Sappho—the incarnation of poetry—and nightingale—the ideal symbol for harmony—represents an idea that poetry could reach the condition of harmony, which both Shao and Swinburne aspire.

Swinburne's influence on Shao took place mainly in the 20s, when Shao had just started his poetic career. This influence never left Shao, but kept being molded by new influence that Shao assimilated. Sitwell entered Shao's horizon in the 30s, with a similar view on nature as Swinburne's. She puts forth the conception of poetry as "the sister of horticulture", that is, each poem grows according to its own nature. However, her notion of horticulture denotes the existence of a garden, a micro-nature with an expectation of guerdon. In comparison, Swinburne's nature is wild and unmanaged, which does not promise any return. Sitwell also comes up with a notion of texture, which could be interpreted as a state of interweave in the union of meaning and sound, or the merging of inner and outer music as Swinburne puts it. Shao's articles certify that he is familiar with Sitwell's conception of texture, which shows the occurrence of influence.

Shao's understanding of Sitwell's texture was also influenced by Qian Zhongshu, as Qian was the first one to pair Sitwell's texture with the Chinese phrase *jili*, a loan word from Weng Fanggang, an 18th-century literary critic. The word *jili* means literally "flesh-grain", and in Weng's conception it is a critical term with an analogy to human physiology. Shao takes in the idea of human physiology and combines it with Sitwell's notion of texture, which leads to an eccentric practice of "the horticulture of sisters".

"The horticulture of sisters" is my term that refers to the rendering where Shao merges flower symbol with a woman's body. Both Sitwell and Shao consider the flower as an incarnation of music. But Shao's flower symbol often has features that allude to female sexual organs, which presents an idiosyncratic union of flower-woman. With the use of texture, Shao s(t)imulates sexual acts through the interaction between the poetic voice and the flower-woman. Sexual consummation with the flower-woman seems to him a way that leads to reproduction, that is, the reproduction of music in poetry.

This unique equation of sexual consummation with the condition of music in poetry suggests the influence of the copulation of Christianity and the conception of horticulture. Shao might not have a univocal system of religious views, but this does not stop him from making synthetic rendering of religious texts. Flower petals are often compared by Shao to female sexual organs, and the falling of petals is linked to the success of sexual consummation, as what comes after the fall of fertilized petals is the stage of reproduction. This is evident in Shao's rendering of the fall of Adam and Eve in the Garden of Eden. This fall starts from the lure of Satan, in the form of a snake, with the bait of songs. Satan/snake is here the embodiment of music, and also the incarnation of the fall: the fall into sexual consummation and the condition of music in poetry. Shao's works also suggest that the woman, who is concurrently the flower, is at the same time Satan/snake and that the sexual consummation with the woman is the means to obtain the condition of music in poetry. There is another way of fall, the fall of flower petals without sexual consummation, which would lead to the withering of the flower and the loss of the condition of music in poetry.

Shao's idea of a woman's body in these flower-women poems is biased and dangerous. He regards a woman's body only as a carrier, an instrument in poetry to yield a condition of music. The significance of this condition of music is equated by Shao with an ecstasy gained from having sexual intercourse with the woman's body. This rendering ignores a woman's agency and disrespects the dignity of a woman's body.

Moore's influence on Shao is more abstract than that of Swinburne and Sitwell. Moore and Shao had personal correspondence, but the influence of Moore did not take shape until Shao's third poetry collection *Twenty-five Poems* came out in 1936. Shao admits that the long gap between *Twenty-five Poems* and his second collection *Flower-like Evil* is due to a creative stagnation where he found his skills as a confinement for his poetry. These skills definitely include the use of texture, which he learned from Sitwell. The deployment of these skills led him to poetic practices that are eccentric yet barren in significance. During this period he was influenced by Moore's practices of prose poetry, an entity that effaces the boundary of prose and verse. Shao's biographies and his similar experiments in prose poetry confirm this influence.

The reason why Moore's influence is abstract lies not in the practice of prose poetry but a conception of pure poetry. Like Swinburne and Sitwell, Moore never builds a systematic theory with well-clarified terms. His notion of pure poetry could only be paraphrased as an exclusion of the poet's personality. This could be further interpreted as the removal of the conception of the body in poetry. This certainly sounds more like an instruction than a definition, for Moore is predominantly more a poetry practitioner than a critic. That being said, this instruction is still vague and abstract. Moore never puts his instructive conception of pure poetry into practice, but Shao takes the manual and attempts to remove the conception of the body in poetry by replacing the dialectic of the body with the dialogic of voices.

This replacement can be best exemplified by a huge change in Shao's attitude towards women. The woman's body, which was once grounded in Shao's poems influenced by Sitwell, and rendered merely as an instrument to produce the condition of music in poetry, is no longer denied her voice as dialogues replace conversations of one man. The removal of the conception of the body frees the woman, the previous instrument, from being the instrumentalized other of "I", and therefore frees music, the entity that was once deemed to be produced by the instrument, from the fixation as something other than poetry.

Moore's conception of pure poetry denotes an ideal, primordial unity of arts. It is where the bodies of various art forms, such as poetry and music, dissolve. However, Shao realizes this state could only be approached indefinitely and never be reached ontologically. Poetry and music, or poetry and other art forms, would always be in a dialogic process with no definite closure. The strategy that he comes up with is to play with the traversing between unity and diversity, that is, between pure poetry and poetry/music.

Just as Eliot observes in "Tradition and the Individual Talent": "No poet, no artist of any art, has his complete meaning alone. His significance, his appreciation is the appreciation of his relation to the dead poets and artists."[6] Shao's idea of the condition of music in poetry could not be comprehended without the examination of the preceding or contemporary writers that influenced him. These influences on Shao are relevant to each other. They form as a dialogue where influence is not one-directional but in a dynamic where the significance of the source of influence would also be altered by the recipient's adaptation. As a poet at the crossroad of cultural exchanges and an important publisher who introduced a profusion of Anglophone and Francophone literature into Republican China, Shao is in a dialogue with a large number of authors. What this book examines is but a small portion of these interesting interconnections. Due to the long marginalization of Shao in twentieth-century literary history, the majority of these interconnections have not been excavated. Therefore further exploration of Shao and the nodes in his influence network will be necessary and rewarding.

One possible direction for further exploration could be to scrutinize other minor influences that help shape Shao's poetics when it comes to the condition of music in poetry. For scholars who are familiar with antiquity and fluent in Latin as well as ancient Greek, Shao's interest in Catullus is worth examining. Shao writes that the poetry of Catullus, as well as Lucretius, is "music flown out from the bottom of heart, needing no adornments and still able to let us feel the beauty of nature" ("真是心底里流出来的音乐，不加修饰而处处能使我们感到自然的美丽").[7] Shao states that Catullus was much influenced by Sappho and that Catullus adores Sappho just as Swinburne does, "as if she's his prelife" ("好像她便是他自己的前身").[8] And speaking of prelife, another interesting figure is Sara Teasdale, which Shao considers as a "modern Sappho" ("近代莎茀").[9] These interconnections are worth investigating.

Another direction is to dwell on Shao's condition of music and its correlation with gender and gender performativity. In his oeuvre, there are many poems that yield a queer reading, as the bodies depicted in these poems seem to allude to a woman at times, and at times someone with a flickering gender. Just as Hohl Trillini observes on Shakespeare's Sonnet 8: "Whatever the 'homosexual truth' in Shakespeare's case, it is undeniable that the effect of identifying the beloved with music is utterly different when the person thus identified is

---

[6] T. S. Eliot, "Tradition and the Individual Talent", *The Sacred Wood: Essays on Poetry and Criticism*, ed. T. S. Eliot (New York: Alfred A. Knopf, 1921), 49.
[7] Shao, "The Love Poems of Catullus", *Collected Works of Shao Xunmei*, 75.
[8] Ibid., 77.
[9] Shao, "Sappho the Greek Sage Poet", *Collected Works of Shao Xunmei*, 183.

male",[10] it might be interesting to see whether the bodies, even the seemingly-woman bodies in Shao's poems are but the performances of a man, or a homunculus in drag. Future works can also investigate the questions such as those proposed by Chancer: "How far have social changes—including, but not limited to, feminism—led men's lives to converge with women's? What common cultural denominators link men's and women's experiences? Where do chasms of misunderstanding and unequal power persist?"[11]

I hope that my book will benefit the scholarship of Shao and contribute to the relevant research in Chinese studies and word and music studies. In the scope of world literature, it is an attempt to fill in a small but important puzzle piece in the global network of literary influence. In a world where cultural exchanges have become increasingly frequent and convenient, and at a time when counter-globalization seems to burgeon into a hazardous trend, it is beneficial and necessary to look back at the period of the 1920s-1930s, a time that is equally tumultuous as today, to examine the global influence network that has taken us where we are, and to understand that in the dynamic of literary influence, no single piece of literature can have its significance alone.

---

[10] Hohl Trillini, *The Gaze of the Listener*, 27.
[11] Lynn S. Chancer, "No More Martians?" *The Women's Review of Books* 2000, vol. 17, no. 7: 19.

Bibliography

Acquisto, Joseph. *French Symbolist Poetry and the Idea of Music*. Burlington: Ashgate, 2006. Print.

Allott, Miriam Farris, ed. *The Brontës: The Critical Heritage*. London: Psychology Press, 1974. Print.

Arnheim, Rudolf. Rev. of *Music and Poetry: The Nineteenth Century and After*. *The Musical Quarterly* 71, no. 3 (1985): 378-381. Print.

Bal, Mieke. "His Master's Eye." *Modernity and the Hegemony of Vision*. Ed. David Michael Levin. Berkeley: University of California Press, 1993. Print.

Bordo, Susan. "Feminist Skepticism and the 'Maleness' of Philosophy." *The Journal of Philosophy* 85, no. 11 (1988): 619-29. Print.

—. "Gay Men's Revenge." *The Journal of Aesthetics and Art Criticism* 57, no. 1 (1999): 21-25. Print.

—. "The Cartesian Masculinization of Thought." *Signs* 11, no. 3 (1986): 439-456. Print.

—. *The Destruction of Hillary Clinton*. London: Melville House, 2017. Print.

—. "The Feminist as Other." *Metaphilosophy* 27, no. 1-2 (1996): 10-27. Print.

—. *The Flight to Objectivity: Essays on Cartesianism and Culture*. New York: SUNY Press, 1987. Print.

—. *Unbearable Weight: Feminism, Western Culture, and the Body*. Berkeley: University of California Press, 1993. Print.

Bradley, A. C. *Oxford Lectures on Poetry*. New Delhi: New Delhi Atlantic Publishers & Dist, 1999. Print.

Chancer, Lynn S. "No More Martians?" *The Women's Review of Books* 17, no. 7 (2000): 18-19. Print.

Chen Yue 陈越. "Zhongguo xiandai shixue zhong de "jilishuo" 中国现代诗学中的"肌理说" ["Texture in Modern Chinese Poetics"]. *Zhongguo xiandai wenxue yanjiu congkan* 中国现代文学研究丛刊 [*Modern Chinese Literature Studies*] no. 3 (2014): 107-121. Print.

Connolly, Thomas E. "Swinburne on 'The Music of Poetry'". *PMLA* 72, no. 4 (1957): 680-688. Print.

Courtney, W. L. *Old Saws and Modern Instances*. 1918. Reprint. London: Forgotten Books, 2013. Print.

Eliot, T. S. "Swinburne as Poet." *The Sacred Wood: Essays on Poetry and Criticism*. Ed. T. S. Eliot. New York: Alfred A. Knopf, 1921. 131-136. Print.

Fruehauf, Heinrich. *Urban Exoticism in Modern Chinese Literature, 1910-1933*. Diss. University of Chicago, 1990. Print.

Gao Wei 高蔚. "Chunshi jiqi zhongguohua yanjiu" 纯诗及其中国化研究 [*A Study of 'Pure Poetry' and Its Reception in China*]. Diss. East China Normal University, 2006. Print.

Gerber, Helmut E. "George Moore: From Pure Poetry to Pure Criticism." *The Journal of Aesthetics and Art Criticism* 25, no. 3 (1967): 281-291. Print.

Green, Lucy *Music, Gender, Education*. Cambridge: Cambridge, 1997. Print.

Han Sheng 韩胜. "Feng Fanggang de shige xuanping yu "jili"shuo de xingcheng 翁方纲的诗歌选评与"肌理"说的形成" [On a Selection of Weng Fanggang's Poetry and the Formation of "Jili"]. *Zhongguo wenxue yanjiu* 中国文学研究 [*Chinese Literature Studies*] no. 3 (2009): 63-71. Print.

Henderson, Philip *Swinburne: The Portrait of a Poet*. London: Routledge & Kegan Paul, 1974. Print.

Hohl Trillini, Regula. *The Gaze of the Listener: English Representations of Domestic Music-Making. Word and Music Studies*, volume 10. New York: Rodopi, 2008. Print.

Hu Shi 胡适. *Changshiji* 尝试集 [A Collection of Attempts]. Beijing: Beijing renmin wenxue chubanshe, 2000. Print.

Huang Zunxian 黄遵宪. *Huang Zunxian shi xuan* 黄遵宪诗选 [An Anthology of [Huang Zunxian]. Beijing: Zhonghua shuju, 2008. Print.

Hutt, Jonathan. "*La Maison D'or* -The Sumptuous World of Shao Xunmei." *East Asian History* no. 21 (2001): 111-142. Print.

Koskoff, Ellen. *A Feminist Ethnomusicology Writings on Music and Gender. New Perspectives on Gender in Music*. Urbana: University of Illinois Press, 2014. Print.

Kramer, Lawrence. *Music and Poetry: The Nineteenth Century and After*. Berkeley; London: University of California Press, 1984. Print.

Lafourcade, Georges. *Swinburne's Hyperion and Other Poems with an Essay on Swinburne and Keats*. London: Faber & Gwyer, 1927. Print.

Lee, Leo. *Shanghai Modern: The Flowering of a New Urban Culture in China*. Cambridge, Mass.; London: Harvard University Press, 1999. Print.

Li Changkong 李长空. "Gelüti xinshi xingshi yu neirong de tongyi" 格律体新诗形式与内容的统一 [Unity of Form and Content in Chinese New Metrical Poetry]. *Jiangsu daxue xuebao (shehuikexueban)* 江苏大学学报 (社会科学版) [Journal of Jiangsu University (Social Science Edition)] no. 2 (2010): 55-59. Print.

Li Guangde 李广德. "Shilun Shao Xunmei de shi yu shilun" 试论邵洵美的诗与诗论 [On the Poetry and Poetics of Shao Xunmei]. *Zhongguo xiandai wenxueyanjiu congshu* 中国现代文学研究丛书 [Modern Chinese Literature Studies] no. 4 (1986): 58-73. Print.

Locker-Lampson, Frederick. *A Selection from the Works of Frederick Locker*. London: Edward Moxon, 1865. Print.

Lu Xun 鲁迅. *Lu Xun quanji* 鲁迅全集 [Complete Works of Lu Xun]. Beijing: Renmin wenxue chubanshe, 2005. Print.

—. *Zhunfengyue tan* 准风月谈 [On Demimonde]. Beijing: Renmin wenxue chubanshe, 1973. Print.

Mao Han 毛翰. "Xinshi gelühua de santiao kexing zhi lu" 新诗格律化的三条可行之路 [Three Possible Ways for the Metricalization of New Poetry]. *Dongnan xueshu* 东南学术 [Southeast Academic Research] no. 1 (2014): 223-232. Print.

McGann, Jerome J. "Wagner, Baudelaire, Swinburne: Poetry in the Condition of Music." *Victorian Poetry* 47, no. 4, "A hundred sleeping years ago": In commemoration of Algernon Charles Swinburne (2009): 619-632. Print.

Moore, George. *Memoirs of My Dead Life*. New York: D. Appleton and Company, 1914. Print.

—. *A Story-Teller's Holiday*. London: Cumann Sean-eolais na hÉireann, 1918. Print.

—. *Avowals*. New York: Boni and Liveright, 1919. Print.

—. *Conversations in Ebury Street*. London: William Heinemann, 1936. Print.

—. *An Anthology of Pure Poetry*. New York: Liveright, 1973. Print.

Moule, A. C., and Paul Pelliot. *Marco Polo: The Description of the World*. London: G. Routledge & Sons, Limited, 1938. Print.

Poe, Edgar Allan. *The Works of Edgar Allan Poe, Vol 3*. London: A&C Black, 1899. Print.

Prieto, Eric. *Listening In: Music, Mind, and the Modernist Narrative*. Lincoln: University of Nebraska Press, 2002. Print.

Qian Zhongshu 钱钟书. *Xiezai rensheng bianshang rensheng bianshang de bianshang shiyu* 写在人生边上 人生边上的边上 石语 [On the Edge of Life, the Edge of the Edge of Life, Stone Talks]. Beijing: Sanlian shudian, 2002. Print.

Qu Qiubai 瞿秋白. *Qu qiubai wenji* 瞿秋白文集 [Works of Qu Qiubai]. Beijing: Renmin wenxue chubanshe, 1953. Print.

Rosenberg, John D. "Swinburne." *Victorian Studies* 11, no. 2 (1967): 131-152. Print.

Russell, Charles E. "Swinburne and Music." *The North American Review* 186, no. 624 (1907): 427-441. Print.

Said, Edward W. *Musical Elaborations*. London: Chatto & Windus, 1991. Print.

Scher, Steven Paul. Rev. of *Music and Poetry: The Nineteenth Century and After*. *19th-Century Music* 10, no. 3 (1987): 290-292. Print.

Shao Xunmei. *Buneng shuohuang de zhiye* 不能说谎的职业 [A Job that Can't Lie]. Shanghai: Shanghai shudian chubanshe, 2012. Print.

—. *Guizuqu* 贵族区 [The Aristocrats' Neighborhood]. Shanghai: Shanghaishudian chubanshe, 2012. Print.

—. *Huayiban de zui'e: Shao Xunmei zuopin xilie shigejuan* 花一般的罪恶: 邵洵美作品系列 诗歌卷 [Flower-like Evil: Poetic Works of Shao Xunmei]. Shanghai: Shanghai shudian chubanshe, 2012. Print.

—. *Huo yu rou* 火与肉 [Fire and Flesh]. Shanghai: Jinwu shudian, 1928. Print.

—. "Jinyao shihua jiuze" 金曜诗话(九则) [Nine Pieces of *Friday on Poetry*]. *Shi tansuo* 诗探索 [Poetry Exploration] no. 1 (2010): 23-36. Print.

—. *Rulin xinshi* 儒林新史 [A New History of Literati]. Shanghai: Shanghai shudian chubanshe, 2012. Print.

—. *The Verse of Shao Xunmei*. Trans. Sun Jicheng 孙继成 and Hal Swindall. Paramus: Homa & Sekey Books, 2016. Print.

—. *Xunmei wencun* 洵美文存 [Collected Works of Shao Xunmei]. Ed. Chen Zishan 陈子善. Shenyang: Liaoning jiaoyu chubanshe, 2006. Print.

—. *Yiduoduo meigui* 一朵朵玫瑰 [Roses and Roses]. Shanghai: Shanghai shudian chubanshe, 2012. Print.

—. *Yigeren de tanhua* 一个人的谈话 [*Conversations of One Man*]. Shanghai: Shanghai shudian chubanshe, 2012. Print.

—. *Ziyoutan* 自由潭 [The Pool of Freedom]. Shanghai: Shanghai shudian chubanshe, 2012. Print.

Shao Xiaohong 邵绡红. *Tiansheng de shiren: wode baba Shao Xunmei* 天生的诗人—我的爸爸邵洵美 [A Natural Born Poet—My Father Shao Xunmei]. Shanghai: Shanghai shudian chubanshe, 2015. Print.

Shen Congwen 沈从文. "Women zenmeyang qudu xinshi" 我们怎么样去读新诗 [How Do We Read New Poetry], in *Zhongguo xiandai shilun shang* 中国现代诗论 上 [Modern Chinese Poetics Volume One]. Ed. Yang Kuanghan 杨匡汉. Guangzhou: Huacheng chubanshe, 1985. Print.

Sheng Xingjun 盛兴军. "Tuifeizhe ji qixinyang—Shao Xunmei yu xifang weimeizhuyi" 颓废者及其信仰—邵洵美与西方"唯美主义" [A Decadent and His Faith—Shao Xunmei and Western Aestheticism]. *Shanghai daxue xuebao* 上海大学学报(社会科学版) [Journal of Shanghai University (Social Science)] 11, no. 1 (2004): 39-45. Print.

Shi Zhecun 施蛰存. "Youguanyu benkanzhong de shi" 又关于本刊中的诗 [About the Poems in the Journal]. *Xiandai* 现代 [Les Contemporains] 4, no. 1 (1933). Print.

Sitwell, Edith. *Aspects of Modern Poetry*. London: Duckworth, 1934. Print.

—. *The Pleasures of Poetry: A Critical Anthology, Second Series, The Romantic Revival*. New York: W. W. Norton and Company, 1934. Print.

—. *Collected Poems*. London: Duckworth Overlook, 2006. Print.

Skerratt, Brian. "Reading Modernity Musically: Zhu Guangqian and the Rhythm of New Poetry", *Chinese Literature: Essays, Articles, Reviews* 2015, vol. 37: 113.

Suleiman, Susan. *The Female Body in Western Culture: Contemporary Perspectives*. London: Harvard University Press, 1985. Print.

Sun Jicheng 孙继成, and Hal Swindall. "A Chinese Swinburne: Shao Xunmei's Life and Art." *The West in Asia and Asia in the West: Essays on Transnational Interactions*. Ed. Elisabetta Marino, Tanfer Emin Tunc. Jefferson: McFarland, 2015. 133-146. Print.

—. "Lun Yingguo shiren Shiwenpeng dui Shao Xunmei shige chuangzuo de yingxiang" 论英国诗人史文朋对邵洵美诗歌创作的影响) [Swinburne's Influence on the Poetry of Shao Xunmei]. *Shandong ligong daxue xuebao (shehuikexue ban)* 山东理工大学学报 (社会科学版) [Journal of Shandong University of Technology (Social Science)] 30, no. 6 (2014): 50-54. Print.

Sung, Ho Yeon. *A Comparative Study of Shao Xunmei's Poetry*. Columbus: Ohio State University Press, 2003. Print.

Swinburne, A. C. *Essays and Studies*. London: Chatto and Windus, 1875. Print.

—. *Poems and Ballads*. London: Chatto and Windus, 1910. Print.

—. *The Poems of Algernon Charles Swinburne*. London: Chatto and Windus, 1904. Print.

—. *William Blake. A Critical Essay*. London: John Camden Hotten, 1868. Print.
Venuti, Lawrence. *The Scandals of Translation: Towards an Ethics of Difference*. New York: Routledge, 1998. Print.
—. *Translation Changes Everything: Theory and Practice*. London: Routledge, 2013. Print.
Wang Jingfang 王京芳. *Shao Xunmei: chubanjie de Tangjikede* 邵洵美: 出版界的堂吉柯德 [Shao Xunmei: Don Quixote in Publishing]. Guangzhou: Guangdong jiaoyu chubanshe, 2012. Print.
Wang Pu 王璞. *Xiangmeili zai Shanghai* 项美丽在上海 [Emily Hahn in Shanghai].Beijing: Renmin wenxue chubanshe, 2005. Print.
Wang Yunxi 王运熙 ed. *Zhongguo wenlunxuan, xiandaijuan (shang)* 中国文论选 现代卷（上）[An Anthology of Chinese Literary Theories, the Modern Volume (1)]. Nanjing: Jiangsu wenyi chubanshe, 1996. Print.
Wen Yiduo 闻一多. "Shi de gelü" 诗的格律 [The Metrics of Poetry]. *Wen yiduo quanji, di er juan* 闻一多全集, 第 2 卷 [Complete Works of Wen Yiduo, vol. 2]. Beijing: Hubei renmin chubanshe (1993), 137-144. Print.
Xie Zhixi 解志熙. *Meide pianzhi* 美的偏至 [The Extreme of Beauty]. Shanghai: Shanghai wenxue chubanshe, 1997. Print.
—. "Yingguo weimeizhuyi wenxue zai xiandai Zhongguo de chuanbo" 英国唯美主义文学在现代中国的传播 [The Dissemination of British Aesthetic Literature in Modern China]. *Waiguo wenxue pinglun* 外国文学评论 [Foreign Literature Review] no.1 (1998): 121-131. Print.
Yue Daiyun 乐黛云. *China and the West at the Crossroads: Essays on Comparative Literature and Culture*. Trans. Geng Song and Darrell Dorrington. Beijing: Springer, 2016. Print.

Index

A

Acquisto, Joseph, xxxix, 113
aestheticism, xxxiv, 116
Aiken, Conrad, xxx
Allott, Miriam Farris, 12, 113
Anglophone, i, v, vii, xii, xvi, xxiv, xxv, xxix, xxxi, xxxii, xxxiii, xxxiv, xxxv, xxxvi, xl, xlvii, xlviii, xlix, 4, 106, 110
Arnheim, Rudolf, xxxviii, 113
Asia, xxxiv, xxxv, 22, 38, 114, 116

B

Bal, Mieke, xliii, xliv, 6, 15, 113, 117
Baudelaire, Charles, xv, xxix, 1, 4, 5, 7, 10, 12, 31, 115
Beardsley, Aubrey, xxix
Bing Xin, xxii
Blake, William, 14, 15, 16, 31, 107, 117
Bordo, Susan, xlvi, xlvii, xlviii, 30, 47, 48, 64, 66, 97, 105, 106, 113
Bradley, A. C., 87, 113

C

Cambridge, xiii, xiv, xviii, xxix, xlii, 1, 2, 3, 6, 16, 20, 34, 52, 114
Candid Comment, xix
Cartesian, xxxvii, xlvii, 64, 113
Celestial Dog Club, xiv
Chancer, Lynn S., 106, 111, 113
Chen Yue, xxxvi, 32, 113
Chen Zishan, xx, xxv, 116

Christian, xii, 52, 53, 54, 108
Christianity, xii, 53, 54, 108
classical Chinese, xx, xxi, xxiii, xxiv, xxvii, xxviii, xxxvi
Communist, xi, xvi, xvii, xviii, xix, 65
Connolly, Thomas E., 11, 13, 14, 15, 113
Courtney, W. L., 6, 7, 113
Crescent Moon Society, xiii, xviii, xxx, 65
Cultural Revolution, xvi

D

Dai Wangshu, xxii
Davies, W. H., xxix, 5
decadent, xxxiv, xxxvii, 116
difference, xlix, 117
Ding Ling, xvii, xix
Dungan Revolt, xi

E

École des Beaux-Arts, xiii, xiv, xxix
Eliot, T. S., 15, 109, 110, 113
Enlightenment, 105
ethnomusicology, xlii, 114

F

female sexual organs, vii, 50, 51, 108
feminist skepticism, xlv, xlvii, 106
Feng Naichao, xxx
Fire and Flesh, xv, xlv, 10, 11, 115

Flower-like Evil, xvi, xxv, l, 10, 66, 83, 109, 115
flower-woman, vii, xlviii, 47, 48, 49, 50, 51, 73, 84, 101, 108
Francophone, xxix, xxxi, xxxiv, xxxv, xl, 4, 110
free verse, xxv, xxvi, xxvii
Fruehauf, Heinrich, xiii, 113

G

Gao Wei, xxxv, 113
Gautier, Théophile, xv, xxix
gaze, xlii, xliii, xliv, 111, 114
gender, xlii, xliv, xlvii, 114
Gerber, Helmut E., 85, 87, 114
Green, Lucy, xlii, 40, 41, 42, 43, 114

H

Hahn, Emily, xvi, xix, xx, 117
haiku, xxiii
Han Sheng, 34, 35, 114
harmony, vii, xlviii, 11, 12, 13, 14, 15, 19, 20, 21, 23, 26, 29, 31, 83, 107
Heaven and May, xv, xxiv, xxv, l, 9, 20
Henderson, Philip, 11, 114
Hohl Trillini, Regula, xlii, xliii, xliv, xlv, 110, 111, 114
Hu Shi, xiii, xx, xxi, xxii, 114
Hu Yepin, xix
Huang Zunxian, xxi, 114
human physiology, vii, 35, 37, 108
Hundred Days' Reform Movement, xx
Hutt, Jonathan, xx, xxxiv, xxxv, 114
Huysmans, Joris-Karl, xxix

I

incarnation, vii, 8, 27, 38, 39, 49, 50, 58, 73, 107, 108
influence, i, v, xxxv, 116
instrumentalized, vii, xlix, 64, 70, 90, 109
interweave, vii, 32, 107

K

Koskoff, Ellen, xlii, 114
Kramer, Lawrence, xxxvii, xxxviii, xl, 114

L

La Maison D'Or Monthly, xiv, xv, xxix, xxxiv, 2, 9, 76
Lafourcade, Georges, 19, 20, 25, 114
Le Chat Noir, xiv
Lee, Leo, xviii, 10, 114
left-wing, xiii, xvii, xviii, xix, 65
Li Changkong, xxvi, 114
Li Guangde, xx, xxxiii, 114
Li Jinfa, xxii
Liang Qichao, xxi
listener, xlii, xliii, xliv, 111, 114
Locker-Lampson, Frederick, 114
Lowell, Amy, xxii
Lu Xun, xvii, xviii, xx, xxii, xxiii, 114

M

Mallarmé, Stéphane, xxix, xxxix
Mao Han, xxvi, xxvii, 115
Mao Zedong, xix
Marxist, xx
May Fourth, xviii, xx, xxiii
McGann, Jerome J., 11, 12, 13, 31, 115

meaning and sound, vii, 14, 15, 20, 21, 26, 29, 32, 107
metrical poetry, xxvi, 114
metricalization, xxvii, 115
metrics, xxvii, 117
Moore, George, vii, xv, xxix, xxxii, xxxiv, xxxv, xxxvii, xliv, xlix, 4, 75, 76, 77, 78, 79, 80, 81, 82, 83, 84, 85, 86, 87, 88, 98, 99, 102, 106, 109, 114, 115
Mrs. Shi, xi
Mu Mutian, xxx
music and poetry, xxxvii, xxxviii, xxxix, xl, 113, 114, 115

N

New Culture Movement, xx, xxi, xxii, xxiii, xxiv, xxv, xxvi, xxviii
New Epoch, xiv
New Poetry, xx, xxi, xxiii, xxiv, xxv, xxvi, xxvii, xxviii, xxxix, 10, 32, 33, 36, 115, 116
nightingale, vii, xxiv, xlv, xlviii, 8, 19, 20, 21, 22, 23, 24, 25, 26, 44, 73, 82, 107

P

Paris, xiii, xiv, xxii, 75, 76
Poe, Edgar Allan, 86, 115
poetics, xxxiii, xxxvi, 10, 32, 35, 37, 81, 113, 114, 116
poetry and music, xxxvii, xlix, 74, 85, 87, 103, 109
Pool of Freedom, xix, l, 30, 116
Pound, Ezra, xxii
Pre-Raphaelites, xxix
Prieto, Eric, xxxix, xl, 115
pure poetry, xxxv, xxxvii, 75, 77, 78, 85, 86, 88, 113, 114, 115

Q

Qian Zhongshu, xxxvi, 33, 34, 108, 115
Qing dynasty, xi, xx
Qu Qiubai, 65, 115
quantitative meter, xxviii

R

reproduction, vii, 39, 49, 51, 64, 108
Republican China, xxxi, xxxiii, xxxiv, xxxv, 9, 32, 65, 110
rhythm, xxviii, xxx, xxxviii, xxxix, 82
Rimbaud, Arthur, xxix
romantic, 12, 29, 31, 32, 33, 89, 116
Rosenberg, John D., 11, 115
Roses and Roses, xv, 3, 10, 16, 39, 40, 41, 116
Russell, Charles E., 13, 14, 115

S

Said, Edward W., xlvi
sapphics, xxviii
Sappho, vii, xv, xxiv, xxv, xxviii, xxxi, xxxii, xxxiv, xliii, xlv, xlviii, 1, 2, 3, 4, 5, 6, 7, 8, 9, 23, 24, 25, 26, 27, 73, 83, 107, 110
Sara Teasdale, xv, xxi
Scher, Steven Paul, xxxvii, xxxviii, xxxix, xli, 115
Second International, xx
sexism, xlvi, 105
sexual consummation, vii, 49, 108
Shanghai, xi, xii, xiv, xvi, xviii, xix, xxv, xxxiv, xxxvi, xxxvii, xli, xlv, 2, 10, 30, 35, 52, 66, 89, 106, 114, 115, 116, 117
Shao Heng, xi

Shao Xiaohong, xi, l, 77, 78, 79, 116
Shao Yi, xi
Shao Youlian, xi
Shao Yunlong, xi
Shao Yunxiang, xvi
Shen Congwen, xiii, xix, 10, 78, 81, 116
Sheng Peiyu, xii, xvi
Sheng Xingjun, xxxiv, 116
Sheng Xuanhuai, xii, xvii
Shi Zhecun, 35, 116
Sitwell, Edith, vii, xxix, xxxii, xxxvi, xxxix, xliv, xlv, xlviii, xlix, 29, 30, 31, 32, 33, 34, 35, 36, 37, 38, 39, 40, 48, 49, 73, 83, 84, 102, 106, 107, 108, 109, 116
Skerratt, Brian, xxv, xxvi, xxvii, 116
Sphinx Club, xiv, xxxiv, 9, 65
Sphinx Fortnightly, xiv, xv, xxix
Sphinx Monthly, xv, xxix
stress variation, xxviii
Suleiman, Susan, 97, 116
Sun Jicheng, xxxv, l, 116
Sung, Ho Yeon, xlv, 116
Swinburne, A. C., vii, xv, xxiv, xxix, xxxii, xxxiii, xxxiv, xxxv, xxxvi, xxxvii, xlv, xlviii, xlix, 1, 6, 7, 8, 9, 10, 11, 12, 13, 14, 15, 19, 20, 21, 22, 23, 24, 25, 26, 27, 29, 31, 32, 38, 39, 40, 41, 65, 73, 83, 84, 106, 107, 109, 110, 113, 114, 115, 116, 117
Swindall, Hal, xx, xxxv, l, 116
syllable weight, xxviii
symbolist poetry, xxxi
Symons, Arthur, xv, xxix

T

tanka, xxiii
Teasdale, Sara, xxi, 41, 110

texture, vii, xxxvi, xxxix, xlviii, 31, 32, 33, 35, 36, 37, 38, 39, 40, 44, 45, 46, 47, 48, 49, 50, 52, 60, 69, 73, 82, 83, 84, 107, 108, 109
the conception of the body, vii, xlix, 81, 87, 88, 99, 109
the condition of music, 12, 31, 115
the dialectic of the body, vii, xliv, xlv, xlix, 88, 109
the dialogic of voices, vii, xliv, xlv, xlix, 88, 109
The Flight to Objectivity, xlvii, 64, 113
The Man, 105, 106
the nineteenth century, xxxvii, xxxviii, xxxix, xl, 113, 114, 115
the sister of horticulture, vii, xlviii, 29, 30, 31, 37, 73, 107
the West, xxxv, 116
translation, xlix, 117
traversing, viii, 98, 99, 103, 109
Tusu, xv, 5, 9, 16
Twenty-five Poems, xvi, xxv, xxviii, l, 83, 109

U

Unbearable Weight, xlvii, 30, 64, 66, 97, 113
unity and diversity, viii, 98, 103, 109
unity of arts, vii, xlix, 103, 109

V

Venuti, Lawrence, xlix, l, 117
Verlaine, Paul, xiv, xv, xxix, 41, 75, 76
Victorian, xxii, 11, 12, 32, 33, 115

W

Wagner, Richard, xl, 12, 31, 115
Wang Duqing, xxx
Wang Jingfang, xx, xxix, 117
Wang Pu, xvi, 117
Wang Yunxi, xxxi, 117
Wen Yiduo, xiii, xxii, xxvii, 117
Weng Fanggang, xxxvi, xlviii, 34, 35, 108, 114
Wenyi Duo, xxii
Wilde, Oscar, xv, xxix
word and music studies, xlii, 114
Wylie, Elinor, xxx

X

Xia Yan, xix
Xie Zhixi, xxxiii, xxxiv, 65, 66, 117
Xu Beihong, xiii
Xu Zhimo, xiii, xxii, 21

Y

Yili, xi
Yu Gengyu, xxx
Yue Daiyun, xxxvi, xxxvii, 117

Z

Zhou Zuoren, xxiii
Zong Baihua, xxii

www.ingramcontent.com/pod-product-compliance
Lightning Source LLC
Chambersburg PA
CBHW052126300426
44116CB00010B/1802